recipes for
GLUTEN-FREE
kids
fun eats from
breakfast to treats!

D1302369

Publications International, Ltd.

Recipe development on pages 24, 30 and 80 by Jen Cafferty.

Recipe development on pages 12, 14, 20, 34, 50, 76, 84, 86, 96, and 106 by Marilyn Pocius.

Contributing writer: Marilyn Pocius

Photography on pages 13, 15, 21, 25, 29, 31, 35, 39, 49, 51, 53, 57, 77, 81, 85, 87, 97, 99, 107 and 121 by PIL Photo Studio.
Photographer: Tate Hunt
Photographer's Assistant: Justin Paris
Food Stylists: Kathy Aragaki, Carol Smoler
Assistant Food Stylists: Sara Cruz, Sheila Grannen

Pictured on the front cover *(clockwise from top right):* Peanutty Crispy Dessert Cups *(page 74),* Kids' Pizzas *(page 78),* Extra-Crunchy Chicken Tenders *(page 30)* and Gluten-Free Waffles *(page 10).*

Pictured on the back cover *(top to bottom):* Ham & Oinks *(page 12),* Chocolate Chip Scones *(page 14)* and Tuna Noodle Bake *(page 50).*

All photographs © Publications International, Ltd. *except* the following: pages 5 and 6 non-food photos by Shutterstock.

Illustrations on page 8 and with chapter titles by Shutterstock. Milk bottle illustration on page 9 by Vector Clip Art.

Microwave Cooking: Microwave ovens vary in wattage. Use the cooking times as guidelines and check for doneness before adding more time.

Note: This book is for informational purposes and is not intended to provide medical advice. Neither Publications International, Ltd., nor the authors, editors or publisher takes responsibility for any possible consequences from any treatment, procedure, exercise, dietary modification, action, or applications of medication or preparation by any person reading or following the information in this cookbook. The publication of this book does not constitute the practice of medicine, and this cookbook does not replace your physician, pharmacist or health-care specialist. **Before undertaking any course of treatment or nutritional plan, the authors, editors and publisher advise the reader to check with a physician or other health-care provider.**

Not all recipes in this cookbook are appropriate for all people with celiac disease, gluten-intolerance, food allergies or sensitivities. Health-care providers and registered dietitians can help design specific meal plans tailored to individual needs.

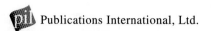 Publications International, Ltd.

contents

introduction

Understanding Gluten

It's not just wheat—gluten is a protein that is found naturally in wheat, rye and barley. It gives structure to the baked goods we know and love. Without it, or something to replace it, bread and cake would be sad little puddles or piles of crumbs. When yeast, baking powder or other leavening agents produce bubbles in a dough or a batter, that air is trapped by the stretchy gluten network and the baked product rises and becomes light.

Eliminating gluten from the food we eat is a lot more complicated than eliminating bread. There is gluten in most of kids' favorite foods—pasta, crackers, bagels, pretzels, pizza, donuts and even chicken nuggets. The good news is that there are many more foods on the gluten-free list than on the forbidden one. There are also more products, from cereals to baking mixes to pastas, that are now being formulated in gluten-free versions. Eating gluten-free can also mean a healthier diet—more fruits and vegetables, less processed food. Play the Gluten Guessing Game below to test your knowledge.

The Gluten Guessing Game

It's hard enough to eliminate the obvious gluten in your life. What makes the journey tougher is that gluten hides in many places you'd never expect. See if you can spot the hidden sources. Answers on page 6.

1 soy sauce	**2** corn bread	**3** tofu	**4** malted milk	**5** turkey gravy
6 hot dogs	**7** kids' dough	**8** corn tortillas	**9** farina	**10** candy

Supermarket Savvy

Before you rush off to buy a cupboard full of specialty products, remember that most basic ingredients are naturally gluten-free. You can pick up any sort of fresh produce, meat or fish without worrying. However, regular macaroni and cheese from a box and fish sticks are no longer on your list. You will want to stock up on some staples so that you're prepared to eat well. Five years ago a health food store was the only place to buy special GF items. Today most supermarkets offer just about everything you need. There are also many reliable online sources that are worth checking out.

The Gluten-Free Pantry

Cooking gluten-free is easier if you keep these staples on hand.

- ❑ beans and lentils
- ❑ chickpea flour
- ❑ corn grits
- ❑ cornmeal and cornstarch
- ❑ corn tortillas and taco shells
- ❑ GF cereal (corn and/or rice)
- ❑ GF flour blends (page 19)
- ❑ GF mixes for your favorite brownies, cookies or muffins
- ❑ GF pasta in various shapes
- ❑ GF soy sauce
- ❑ polenta
- ❑ quinoa
- ❑ rice (arborio rice, basmati rice, wild rice)
- ❑ rice flour (brown, white and sweet rice flour)
- ❑ rice noodles
- ❑ tapioca flour
- ❑ wild rice
- ❑ xanthan gum

Happy Healthy Gluten-Free Kids

How do you explain to your child that he or she can't have a piece of Johnny's birthday cake or that those chocolate chip cookies that smell so good are off limits? It sounds impossible. Most parents would much rather make sacrifices themselves than ask their children to make them. Kids are, fortunately, considerably more resilient than we think and a gluten-free lifestyle has many positive benefits even from a pint-size perspective. Chances are this change in diet is going to be a lot harder on you than on your child.

You Are Not Alone

See your doctor and make sure the right tests are done for celiac disease, gluten-intolerance and any other food sensitivities. Celiac does run in families, so if you or a close relative has the disease, it's more likely that others do as well. Seek out local support groups or search online for information and assistance in raising your gluten-free child.

Make it Positive

Children pick up on adult attitudes and emotions (at least until they are teenagers!). They are also quite adept at knowing when you are trying to convince them of something you don't believe. Just try to make your kid eat broccoli if you loathe it yourself! You need to appreciate the benefits of living gluten-free first. The major plus is better health now and for the future. Many symptoms will improve almost immediately. Help your child understand that the reason his tummyaches went away is that he is now gluten-free. Instead of focusing on what is forbidden, emphasize the delicious gluten-free good things on the menu. Once they see photos of the yummy treats in this book, your kids may even volunteer to help you cook!

Answers: Numbers 2, 4, 5, 7 and 9 contain gluten. Numbers 3 and 8 do NOT contain gluten. Numbers 1, 6 and 10 are "maybes."

Number 1: Soy sauce is usually made with wheat; however some brands are gluten-free and tamari (Japanese soy sauce) often is, but check ingredients.

Number 6: Most, but NOT all, hot dogs and other sausages are gluten-free. Once again, it's important to check the labels.

Number 10: Most candy is gluten-free, but check carefully. Gluten can be used to thicken candy or to make it crispy.

Ten Tips to Ease the Way

I. Give Them Control. The more your child understands the GF diet and the reasons for it, the better. Sooner or later he will have to make decisions when you're not around.

2. Spread the Word. Make baby-sitters, friends' parents, relatives and school officials aware that your child is on the GF diet and that it is extremely important he sticks to it.

3. Explain How to Explain. It can be something simple, like "I'm allergic to gluten." The more a child feels comfortable talking about dietary restrictions, the safer he is.

4. Home Work. Keep your kitchen safe from cross-contamination. Make it easy for your child to find delicious and nutritious gluten-free snacks.

5. Find Alternatives. You will not be able to replace brownies with broccoli. Instead bake Rocky Road Brownies (page 120) or offer another gluten-free treat.

6. Party Plan. If your son or daughter is invited to a birthday party or sleepover, send along a gluten-free replacement for whatever is being served. Explain the situation to the parent in charge and let them know what you're sending.

7. School Daze. Ask the teacher to keep a stash of gluten-free goodies on hand so when there's a celebration involving food, he won't feel left out.

8. Lunch Breaks. What lunch looks like is important. Other kids can be mean and make fun of food that looks different. Consult with your child for help in creating a safe but "cool" lunch.

9. Use Mistakes. We all make them. If your child accidentally (or on purpose) eats gluten, don't berate him. If eating it made him feel lousy, though, point it out.

IO. Don't Make it a Big Deal. It is a big deal for you, but a kid's world is filled with friends, pets, bikes, superheroes and recess. They are probably not obsessing about food like you are, and that's good.

Dairy-Free and Gluten-Free: The GFCF Diet

Many families are choosing a gluten-free casein-free (GFCF) diet for children with symptoms of ADD/ADHD or autism. While there is no scientific evidence that eliminating gluten and casein helps these conditions, there are many anecdotal accounts of improvements in symptoms. Why would this be so? One theory is that some children are not able to completely digest the protein in milk (casein) and wheat (gluten) and that these leftover proteins form peptides in the blood that act like opiates in the body, influencing behavior. Research in the U.S. and Europe has found peptides in the urine of a significant number of children with autism.

Nondairy is NOT Always Dairy-Free

Many products labeled nondairy contain whey, casein or other milk-derived ingredients. According to the FDA, nondairy products can contain 0.5% or less of milk products by weight. Nondairy creamers and nondairy whipped toppings usually contain dairy in some form.

Studies are currently underway to see if the GFCF diet really can be proven effective. Always consult your doctor before changing your child's diet. Tests can determine sensitivities to gluten and casein and whether there are peptides present. You should also get professional dietary advice to ensure your child will be getting the nutrition he or she needs.

What Is Casein?

Casein is the primary protein in milk. (Lactose is milk sugar. It is possible to be lactose intolerant but able to handle casein, though often when one is problematic they both are.) What complicates a GFCF diet is the fact that casein is used as a binding agent in many processed foods and goes by many different chemical names.

Cooking Minus the Moo

Clearly milk, cheese and butter are off the ingredient list, but did you know that most margarine contains dairy in the form of whey or casein? So do many soy cheeses. Fortunately, U.S. food manufacturers are now required to list the simple word "milk" as part of the ingredient list or in boldface type at the end of the list, even if the actual ingredient goes by an obscure chemical name. The recent popularity of the vegan diet is a boon for dairy-free shoppers, too. Since vegans consume no animal products, you can assume products labeled vegan are dairy-free. The kosher designation "pareve" is another handy indicator that the product contains no milk.

Dairy Doubles

The good news is that there are better dairy replacement products available all the time. In addition to soymilk, you can purchase almond milk, rice milk, oat milk and even hemp milk. For most recipes dairy-free milk may be substituted one-for-one for cow's milk. You may want to choose one kind of milk for drinking and another for cooking. Vanilla soymilk is delicious on its own but would be quite odd in mashed potatoes!

To replace butter in most baking recipes, choose a stick form of dairy-free margarine. Dairy-free spreads sold in tubs will not always work well in baking recipes because of the softer consistency.

Cheese is one of the toughest things to replace. Some dairy-free cheeses taste nothing like the real thing and many of them melt poorly or not at all, but there are more and better choices all the time. For bland cheeses, like ricotta or cottage cheese, crumbled tofu is often a good stand in.

How to Use This Book

While all the recipes in this book are gluten-free, there are many sources of hidden gluten and also a range of sensitivities. If your child is very sensitive be careful of ingredients that are gluten- or dairy-free, but processed in a facility that also handles wheat or milk.

A special dairy-free icon marks dairy-free recipes in this book. **dairy-free** Be sure to double-check all ingredients before beginning a recipe. Remember that product formulations can change over time, too. When in doubt, check with the manufacturer of the product.

Where Gluten-Free All-Purpose Flour Blend is listed as an ingredient, the following recipe was used.

gluten-free all-purpose flour blend

(This blend is for all baked goods not made with yeast.)

1 cup white rice flour
1 cup sorghum flour
1 cup tapioca flour
1 cup cornstarch
1 cup almond flour or coconut flour

Combine all ingredients in a large bowl. Whisk to make sure the flours are evenly distributed. The recipe can be doubled or tripled. Store in an airtight container in the refrigerator.

gluten-free waffles

   2 eggs
½ cup plain yogurt
½ cup milk
   1 cup Gluten-Free All-Purpose Flour Blend (page 9)
   1 tablespoon sugar
   1 teaspoon baking powder
   1 teaspoon baking soda
½ teaspoon salt
   2 tablespoons butter, melted
      Butter and syrup

1. Preheat waffle iron according to manufacturer's directions.

2. Beat eggs in large bowl until light and fluffy. Whisk in yogurt and milk. Combine flour blend, sugar, baking powder, baking soda and salt in medium bowl.

3. Gradually whisk yogurt mixture into flour mixture until smooth. Whisk in melted butter.

4. Add batter to waffle iron by ½ cupfuls for 6-inch waffles (or adjust amount depending on waffle iron). Bake until crisp and browned. Serve with butter and syrup. Refrigerate or freeze leftover waffles and reheat in toaster oven until crisp.   **Makes 5 (6-inch) waffles**

ham & oinks

dairy-free

2 teaspoons dairy-free margarine or olive oil
2 eggs
2 crisp corn tostada shells*
 Salt and black pepper
¼ cup shredded dairy-free cheese alternative (optional)
 2 round deli ham slices, plus additional for decoration
 Tomato slices
 Squeezable yellow mustard

If prepared tostada shells are not available, crisp regular corn tortillas by brushing with oil and baking in 350°F oven for 10 to 15 minutes.

1. Heat oil in small nonstick skillet over medium low heat. Add eggs; season with salt and pepper. Scramble 2 to 3 minutes until firm.

2. Place tostada shells on serving plates. Divide egg mixture between tostada shells. Top eggs with shredded cheese, if desired. Arrange ham slices over eggs. Cut additional ham into triangle shapes for ears. Place oval tomato slice for nose. Use mustard to draw eyes and mouth.

Makes 2 servings

tip

Finding a replacement for cheese may be the biggest challenge for those on a dairy-free diet. It's important to read labels carefully since many soy cheeses do contain dairy in the form of casein or whey. Flavors vary, too, and many dairy-free cheeses simply will not melt. Try different brands until you find one you like.

chocolate chip scones

2 cups Gluten-Free All-Purpose Flour Blend, plus additional for work surfaces (page 9)
¼ cup sugar
2½ teaspoons baking powder
¾ teaspoon salt
¾ teaspoon xanthan gum
½ teaspoon baking soda
1 cup semisweet chocolate chips, divided
½ cup (1 stick) cold butter, cut into small pieces
¾ cup milk
½ cup plain yogurt

1. Preheat oven to 425°F.

2. Combine flour blend, sugar, baking powder, salt, xanthan gum and baking soda in large bowl. Add ½ cup chocolate chips and toss to combine.

3. Cut butter into flour mixture with pastry blender or two knives until coarse crumbs form. Stir milk into yogurt in medium bowl until combined.

4. Gradually add yogurt mixture to flour mixture. Stir together just until dough begins to form. (You may not need all of yogurt mixture.) Transfer to surface sprinkled with flour blend. Knead 5 or 6 times until dough holds together. Divide into 3 pieces.

5. Pat each dough piece into circle about ½ inch thick. Cut each circle into 6 wedges with floured knife. Transfer scones to baking sheet; space 2 inches apart.

6. Bake 10 to 14 minutes or until lightly browned. Cool on wire rack. Meanwhile, melt remaining ½ cup chocolate chips in small bowl. Drizzle over scones. **Makes 18 scones**

apple pancakes

dairy-free

2 tablespoons plus 2 teaspoons dairy-free stick margarine
1¼ cups soymilk or other dairy-free milk
2 eggs, beaten
1¼ cups Gluten-Free All-Purpose Flour Blend (page 9)
¼ cup finely chopped dried apple
¼ cup golden raisins
3 tablespoons sugar
1 tablespoon baking powder
1 teaspoon ground cinnamon
½ teaspoon salt
  Maple syrup and additional dairy-free margarine

1. Melt margarine in large skillet or griddle over medium heat. Pour into medium bowl, leaving thin film of margarine on skillet. Whisk soymilk and eggs into margarine in bowl.

2. Combine flour blend, apple, raisins, sugar, baking powder, cinnamon and salt in large bowl. Add soymilk mixture; stir to combine.

3. Pour ¼ cup batter into skillet for each pancake. Cook over medium heat 2 to 3 minutes on each side or until golden. Serve with maple syrup.

Makes 10 to 12 pancakes

breakfast pom smoothie

dairy-free

1 small ripe banana
½ cup mixed berries
¾ cup pomegranate juice
⅓ to ½ cup soymilk or milk

Combine banana and berries in blender; process until smooth. Add juice and soymilk; process until smooth. Serve immediately.

Makes 2 servings

blueberry coconut flour muffins

    6 eggs
    ¼ cup (½ stick) butter, melted
    ¼ cup milk
    ½ cup sugar
    ½ cup plus 2 teaspoons coconut flour,* divided
    2 teaspoons grated lemon peel
    ½ teaspoon salt
    ½ teaspoon baking powder
    ½ teaspoon xanthan gum
    1 cup blueberries

Coconut flour is a gluten-free, high-fiber flour available in the specialty flour section of many supermarkets. It can also be ordered on the internet.

1. Preheat oven to 375°F. Grease 12 standard (2¾-inch) muffin cups or line with paper liners.

2. Whisk eggs, butter, milk and sugar in medium bowl until well combined.

3. Thoroughly combine ½ cup coconut flour, lemon peel, salt, baking powder and xanthan gum in medium bowl. Sift flour mixture into egg mixture. Whisk until batter is smooth.

4. Combine blueberries with remaining 2 teaspoons coconut flour in small bowl. Stir gently into batter.

5. Fill prepared muffin cups almost full. Bake 12 to 15 minutes or until toothpick inserted into centers comes out clean. Cool on wire rack 5 minutes. Remove from pan; serve warm.   **Makes 12 muffins**

dairy-free variation: Replace butter with dairy-free stick margarine and milk with soymilk or other dairy-free milk.

egg in a hole with a hat

 dairy-free

- **2 corn tortillas**
- **1 tomato, diced**
- **1 avocado, diced**
- **¼ teaspoon salt**
- **¼ teaspoon black pepper**
- **¼ teaspoon cumin**
- **Pinch ground red pepper**
- **2 teaspoons olive oil**
- **2 eggs**

1. Cut round hole in center of tortilla using 3-inch cookie cutter. Combine tomato, avocado, salt, pepper, cumin and red pepper in small bowl.

2. Heat large skillet or griddle over medium-low heat; brush with olive oil. Place tortillas in skillet and break one egg into center of each hole. Cook 2 to 3 minutes or until whites have firmed. Carefully flip tortilla and egg and cook to desired doneness. Warm tortilla cut-outs in skillet.

3. Serve tortilla and egg with tomato avocado mixture and top with tortilla cut-out "hats."

Makes 2 servings

fruit kabobs with raspberry yogurt dip

 dairy-free

- **½ cup dairy-free plain soy yogurt or other dairy-free yogurt**
- **¼ cup raspberry fruit spread**
- **1 pint fresh strawberries**
- **2 cups cubed honeydew melon (1-inch cubes)**
- **2 cups cubed cantaloupe (1-inch cubes)**
- **1 can (8 ounces) pineapple chunks in juice, drained**

Combine yogurt and fruit spread in small bowl until well blended. Thread fruit alternately onto six 12-inch wooden skewers. Serve with dip.

Makes 6 servings

corny critters

 dairy-free

1 cup cornmeal
1 tablespoon sugar
½ teaspoon salt
1 cup boiling water
½ cup Gluten-Free All-Purpose Flour Blend (page 9)
½ cup soymilk or other dairy-free milk
1 egg, beaten
2 tablespoons dairy-free margarine, melted
2 teaspoons baking powder
  Dried apricots
  Sliced almonds

1. Combine cornmeal, sugar and salt in medium bowl. Stir in boiling water. Cover; let rest 10 minutes.

2. Stir flour blend, soymilk, egg, margarine and baking powder into cornmeal until smooth.

3. Heat large nonstick skillet or griddle over medium heat. Brush lightly with oil. Transfer some of batter to measuring cup with pour spout. Cut apricots into shapes for noses, mouths and whiskers.

4. Pour small circles of batter onto skillet; drizzle additional batter to make puppy or bunny ears. Use a knife to straighten edges of batter as needed. Add almond eyes with dried cranberry pupils. Place pieces of dried apricot for noses and mouths. Press into batter.

5. Cook 2 to 3 minutes until bubbles appear on top of pancakes and edges become dull. Turn carefully with spatula sprayed with nonstick cooking spray. Cook 1 to 2 minutes or until lightly browned on both sides. Serve pancakes with syrup, if desired.

Makes about 4 servings (10 to 12 pancakes)

bacon & egg cups

12 slices bacon, crisp-cooked and cut crosswise into thirds
6 eggs or 1½ cups egg substitute
½ cup diced bell pepper
½ cup (2 ounces) shredded pepper jack cheese
½ cup half-and-half
¼ teaspoon salt
¼ teaspoon black pepper

1. Preheat oven to 350°F. Lightly spray 12 standard (2½-inch) muffin cups with nonstick cooking spray.

2. Place 3 bacon slices in each prepared muffin cup, overlapping on bottom. Beat eggs, bell pepper, cheese, half-and-half, salt and black pepper in medium bowl until well blended. Fill each muffin cup with ¼ cup egg mixture.

3. Bake 20 to 25 minutes or until eggs are set in center. Run knife around edge of each cup before removing from pan.   **Makes 12 servings**

If someone in your family is allergic to eggs, be aware
that most products labeled egg substitute are made of
egg whites. It eliminates cholesterol, but is certainly not
appropriate for anyone with an egg allergy.

applesauce muffins

dairy-free

2 cups Gluten-Free All-Purpose Flour Blend (page 9)
½ cup plus 3 tablespoons granulated sugar, divided
½ cup plus 3 tablespoons packed brown sugar, divided
4 teaspoons cinnamon, divided
2 teaspoons baking powder
1 teaspoon baking soda
1 teaspoon xanthan gum
½ cup chunky applesauce
½ cup vegetable oil
½ cup apple cider
2 eggs
3 tablespoons dairy-free margarine
Powdered sugar (optional)

1. Preheat oven to 350°F. Line 16 standard (2½-inch) muffin cups with paper baking cups.

2. Combine flour blend, ½ cup granulated sugar, ½ cup brown sugar, 3 teaspoons cinnamon, baking powder, baking soda and xanthan gum in large bowl. Add applesauce, oil, apple cider and eggs; mix well.

3. For topping, stir together remaining 3 tablespoons granulated sugar, 3 tablespoons brown sugar, 1 teaspoon cinnamon and margarine with fork until small clumps form.

4. Fill prepared muffin cups two-thirds full with batter. Sprinkle with topping. Bake on center rack 25 to 30 minutes. Cool 5 minutes in pan on wire rack; remove from pan to cool completely. Dust tops with powdered sugar.

Makes 16 muffins

banana split breakfast bowl

 dairy-free

2½ tablespoons sliced almonds
2½ tablespoons chopped walnuts
3 cups vanilla soy yogurt or other dairy-free yogurt
1⅓ cups sliced strawberries (about 12 medium)
2 bananas, sliced
½ cup drained pineapple tidbits

1. Spread almonds and walnuts in single layer in small heavy skillet. Cook and stir over medium heat 2 minutes or until nuts are lightly browned. Immediately remove from skillet; let cool before using.

2. Divide yogurt among 4 bowls. Layer strawberries, banana slices and pineapple on top. Sprinkle with almonds and walnuts.

Makes 4 servings

Breakfast is a great time to eat one of the two recommended fruit servings for the day. This recipe can be made with frozen strawberries or other fruit. Frozen fruits are picked at their peak and can be stored in the freezer until the date on the package or up to 12 months at 0°F. While fresh can be better, frozen fruits are economical, nutritious, ready to use and available year-round.

hip hop hash

dairy-free

- 1 tablespoon dairy-free margarine
- 1 tablespoon sweet rice flour (mochiko)*
- ⅓ cup beef broth
- 1 teaspoon Worcestershire sauce
- 1 pound prepared beef pot roast, diced
- 1 medium sweet potato (about 12 ounces) peeled and diced
- 1 stalk celery, diced
- 1 cup corn
- ¼ cup diced red or green bell pepper

Sweet rice flour is often labeled mochiko (the Japanese term). It is available in the Asian section of large supermarkets, at Asian grocery stores and online.

1. Melt margarine in large skillet over medium heat; whisk in rice flour and cook 2 minutes, stirring constantly. Whisk in broth and Worcestershire sauce; bring to a simmer. Add beef, potato, celery, corn and bell pepper.

2. Return to a simmer; cover, and cook 12 minutes or until vegetables are tender. **Makes 4 servings**

extra crunchy chicken tenders

2 cups gluten-free corn flakes
1 cup gluten-free pretzels
½ teaspoon garlic powder
⅛ teaspoon paprika
⅛ teaspoon mustard powder
1 cup Gluten-Free All-Purpose Flour Blend (page 9)
1 teaspoon salt
½ teaspoon ground black pepper
3 eggs, lightly beaten
1 teaspoon gluten-free soy sauce
1 pound chicken tenders
Nonstick cooking spray
Barbecue sauce or honey mustard (optional)

1. Preheat oven to 350°F. Combine corn flakes and pretzels in food processor; pulse until coarse crumbs form.

2. Pour crumbs in shallow dish; stir in garlic powder, paprika and mustard powder. Combine flour blend, salt and black pepper in another shallow dish. Combine eggs and soy sauce in third shallow dish.

3. Coat chicken with seasoned flour blend; shake off excess. Dip in egg mixture; drain. Transfer to crumb mixture; coat both sides with crumbs.

4. Spray large nonstick skillet with cooking spray. Working in batches brown chicken on both sides; transfer to large cookie sheet.

5. Bake 10 minutes or until chicken is cooked through. Serve with barbecue sauce or honey mustard for dipping.   **Makes 4 to 6 servings**

chili con corny

1 tablespoon vegetable oil
½ cup finely chopped onion
1 pound ground turkey
1 can (about 15 ounces) kidney beans, rinsed and drained
1 can (about 14 ounces) diced tomatoes
1 can (11 ounces) corn, drained
1 can (8 ounces) tomato sauce
2 teaspoons gluten-free chili powder
1 teaspoon salt
1 teaspoon ground cumin
¾ cup (3 ounces) shredded Cheddar cheese
2 cups corn chips

1. Heat oil in large skillet over medium heat. Add onion; cook and stir 2 minutes. Add turkey; cook until no longer pink, stirring to break up meat.

2. Stir in beans, tomatoes, corn, tomato sauce, chili powder, salt and cumin. Bring mixture to a simmer; cook 10 minutes, stirring frequently.

3. Divide chili among 4 serving bowls. Sprinkle with cheese and top with corn chips. **Makes 4 servings**

dairy-free variation: Omit the Cheddar cheese or substitute your favorite dairy-free cheese alternative.

pb joe & jane

dairy-free

2 rice cakes
2 tablespoons smooth peanut butter
1 red apple
   Grape, apricot or cherry preserves
   Grapes or raisins

Place rice cakes on flat work surface. Spread with peanut butter. Decorate to make faces. Cut apple into short sticks for Jane's hair. Cut apple into curved pieces for mouths. Make Joe's hair with preserves. For eyes, slice grape into quarters or use raisins.   **Makes 2 servings**

jerk "dino" strips

dairy-free

¼ cup dairy-free mayonnaise
2 tablespoons orange marmalade or orange fruit spread
1 tablespoon fresh lime juice
1 teaspoon sugar
¼ teaspoon salt
¼ teaspoon ground ginger
¼ teaspoon garlic salt
¼ teaspoon black pepper
⅛ teaspoon ground red pepper
1 pound boneless chicken breast strips

1. Prepare grill for direct cooking. For dip, combine mayonnaise and orange marmalade in small bowl; set aside.

2. Combine lime juice, sugar, salt, ginger, garlic salt, black pepper and red pepper in shallow bowl. Roll chicken strips in seasoning mixture. Let stand 5 minutes to absorb seasonings.

3. Grill chicken in grill basket over high heat 3 to 4 minutes per side or until cooked through. Serve with dip.   **Makes 4 servings**

meat loaf cupcakes

 dairy-free

  3 medium potatoes, peeled and chopped
1½ pounds 90% lean ground beef
  ½ cup finely chopped onion
  ⅓ cup gluten-free corn or rice cereal squares, crushed
   1 egg
  2 tablespoons chopped fresh rosemary
  ½ cup soymilk or other dairy-free milk
  2 tablespoons dairy-free margarine
  1 teaspoon salt
     Black pepper
  ¼ cup snipped fresh chives

I. Preheat oven to 350°F. Place potatoes in medium saucepan; cover with water. Bring to a boil; cook 25 to 30 minutes or until potatoes are fork-tender.

2. Meanwhile, combine beef, onion, cereal, egg and rosemary in large bowl; mix well. Divide mixture among 10 standard (2½-inch) muffin cups or silicone baking cups. Bake 25 minutes or until cooked through (160°F).

3. Beat potatoes, soymilk, margarine, salt and pepper in large bowl with electric mixer at medium speed 3 minutes or until smooth. Place mashed potato mixture in large piping bag fitted with large star tip.

4. Remove meat loaf cupcakes to serving platter. Pipe mashed potatoes on top for frosting. Sprinkle with chives.   **Makes 10 servings**

tip

If you don't have a piping bag or just don't want to take the time, frost the cupcakes with the mashed potatoes as you would any other cupcakes. In fact, you could enlist the kids to do the frosting and in this case it's fine to let them lick the spoon!

beanie weenies

 dairy-free

1 can (about 15 ounces) light red kidney or pinto beans, rinsed and drained
1 cup frozen corn kernels
½ cup mild salsa
2 tablespoons water
2 teaspoons gluten-free taco seasoning
4 gluten-free hot dogs, sliced
   Corn chips or corn tortillas

1. Combine beans, corn, salsa, water and taco seasoning in large skillet; mix well. Bring to a simmer over medium heat.

2. Stir in hot dogs; cook about 5 minutes or until heated through. Serve with corn chips.

Makes 4 servings

Sure, you know that hot dog buns aren't gluten-free, but it might be a surprise to find that hot dogs and sausages often contain gluten and dairy products, too. Both wheat and milk products are sometimes added to improve the texture and taste of sausage. Read labels carefully and consult the manufacturer if in doubt. The good news is that more and more companies are offering hot dogs without gluten or casein as awareness of the thousands of children with dietary restrictions increases.

italian vegetable soup

 dairy-free

1 tablespoon olive oil
1 medium red onion, chopped
1 medium red bell pepper, chopped
3 cans (about 14 ounces each) chicken broth
1 package (16 ounces) frozen Italian vegetables or mixed vegetables
1 can (about 15 ounces) chickpeas, rinsed and drained
1 can (about 14 ounces) diced tomatoes
1 teaspoon dried oregano
½ teaspoon salt
½ teaspoon black pepper
1 cup diced cooked chicken (optional)

1. Heat oil in Dutch oven. Add onion and bell pepper. Cook and stir over medium-high heat 3 minutes or until onion is tender. Stir in broth, frozen vegetables, chickpeas, tomatoes, oregano, salt and black pepper. Bring to a boil over high heat.

2. Stir in chicken, if desired. Reduce heat to medium; simmer 15 minutes or until vegetables are tender. **Makes 6 servings**

For convenient school lunches, cool soup and pack into freezer containers. Label and freeze. Transfer soup from freezer to refrigerator the night before. In the morning, heat soup in the microwave until piping hot. Preheat vacuum container with boiling water; drain and dry. Pour soup into vacuum container and seal.

california ham rolls

 dairy-free

2 cups water
½ teaspoon salt, divided
1 cup short grain brown rice
2 tablespoons Asian rice vinegar* or cider vinegar
1 tablespoon sugar
4 (8-inch) sheets toasted nori (sushi wrappers)*
8 thin strips ham (about 4 ounces)
¼ cup gluten-free soy sauce
1 tablespoon minced chives

*These ingredients can be found in the ethnic section of most supermarkets.

I. Bring water and ¼ teaspoon salt to a boil in medium saucepan over high heat. Stir in rice. Cover; reduce heat to low. Simmer 40 to 45 minutes or until water is absorbed and rice is tender but chewy. Spoon rice into large shallow bowl.

2. Combine vinegar, sugar and remaining ¼ teaspoon salt in small bowl. Microwave on HIGH 30 seconds. Stir to dissolve sugar. Pour over rice; stir to mix well. Set aside to cool.

3. Place 1 sheet of nori on work surface. Loosely spread about ½ cup of rice over nori, leaving ½-inch border. Place 2 strips of ham along width of nori. Tightly roll up. Gently press to redistribute rice, if necessary. Cut roll into 6 slices with sharp knife. Place cut side up on serving plate. Repeat with remaining nori, rice and ham.

4. Serve soy sauce in small bowl sprinkled with chives for dipping.

Makes 4 servings

surfin' salmon

⅓ cup gluten-free cornflake crumbs
1 egg
2 tablespoons milk
¾ teaspoon dried dill weed
⅛ teaspoon black pepper
  Dash hot pepper sauce
1 can (about 14 ounces) salmon, drained and skin and bones removed
  Nonstick cooking spray
1 teaspoon olive oil
6 tablespoons tartar sauce
5 small pimiento pieces

1. Combine cornflake crumbs, egg, milk, dill, black pepper and hot pepper sauce in large bowl. Add salmon; mix well.

2. Shape salmon mixture into 5 large egg-shaped balls. Flatten each ball into ¾-inch-thick oval. Pinch one end of each oval to make tail shape.

3. Spray large nonstick skillet with cooking spray. Cook fish over medium-high heat 2 to 3 minutes per side or until firm and lightly browned. Turn fish over, adding oil to skillet as necessary to prevent sticking and increase browning.

4. Place small drop of tartar sauce and pimiento on each fish to make "eye." Serve with remaining tartar sauce.   **Makes 5 servings**

serving suggestion: For a tasty side dish of "sea plants," serve fish on a bed of shredded Romaine lettuce and matchstick-size cucumber slices.

dairy-free variation: Replace milk with soymilk or other dairy-free milk. Instead of tartar sauce, use dairy-free tartar sauce or dairy-free mayonnaise.

bacon-wrapped bbq chicken

 dairy-free

> 8 chicken tenders (about 1 pound)
> ½ teaspoon paprika or cumin (optional)
> 8 slices bacon
> ½ cup barbecue sauce, divided

1. Preheat broiler. Line broiler pan with foil.

2. Sprinkle chicken tenders with paprika, if desired. Wrap each chicken tender with slice of bacon in spiral pattern; place on prepared pan.

3. Broil chicken 4 minutes. Turn and broil 2 minutes. Brush with ¼ cup barbecue sauce; broil 2 minutes. Turn and brush with remaining ¼ cup barbecue sauce; broil 2 minutes or until chicken is no longer pink in center.

Makes 4 servings

ranchero roll-ups

 dairy-free

> 4 soft corn tortillas
> ½ cup refried beans, warmed
> 1 large avocado, sliced
> ¼ cup gluten-free enchilada sauce or tomatillo salsa

1. Heat tortillas in microwave 20 to 30 seconds until softened.

2. Spread tortillas with beans; top with avocado and sauce. Roll up and serve.

Makes 2 to 4 servings

sandwich bread

 dairy-free

3 cups Gluten-Free Flour Blend for Breads (recipe follows)
2 packages (¼ ounce each) active dry yeast
2 teaspoons xanthan gum
1 teaspoon salt
1 cup warm water, plus additional as needed
¼ cup vegetable oil
2 eggs, at room temperature
1 tablespoon honey
1 teaspoon cider vinegar

1. Line 9×5-inch loaf pan with foil dull side out. (Do not use glass loaf pan.) Extend sides of foil 3 inches up from top of pan. Spray with nonstick cooking spray and sprinkle with flour blend.

2. Mix 3 cups flour blend, yeast, xanthan gum and salt in large bowl. Whisk 1 cup water, oil, eggs, honey and vinegar together in medium bowl. Beat into dry ingredients with electric mixer at low speed until batter is smooth, shiny and thick. Add more water by tablespoonfuls if needed. Turn mixer to medium-high. Beat batter 5 minutes, scraping bowl occasionally.

3. Spoon batter into prepared pan. Cover with lightly oiled plastic wrap. Let rise in warm place 30 minutes or until batter reaches top of pan.

4. Preheat oven to 375°F. Bake 30 to 35 minutes or until bread sounds hollow when tapped and internal temperature is 200°F. Remove from pan and cool on wire rack. **Makes 1 loaf**

gluten-free flour blend for breads: Combine 1 cup brown rice flour, 1 cup sorghum flour, ¾ cup millet flour, 1 cup tapioca flour, 1 cup cornstarch and ⅓ cup instant mashed potato flakes in large bowl. Whisk thoroughly; store in airtight container in refrigerator.

porkie packs

dairy-free

2 teaspoons seasoned salt
¼ teaspoon black pepper
1½ pounds pork tenderloin
½ cup barbecue sauce
1 large sweet potato, peeled and thinly sliced
1½ cups cooked brown rice
2 medium zucchini, sliced
1 red bell pepper, cut into strips

1. Preheat oven to 450°F. Mix seasoned salt with black pepper on large plate. Dry tenderloin with paper towel; roll in seasoning mix to coat. Cut tenderloin crosswise into ½-inch slices.

2. Place 6 sheets of heavy-duty foil on work surface. Spoon about 2 teaspoons of barbecue sauce onto each sheet, slightly off-center. Divide pork slices among sheets, placing on sauce. Brush pork with additional 2 teaspoons of sauce.

3. Top pork evenly with sweet potato, rice, zucchini and bell pepper. Fold foil loosely to make packets and seal edges with overlapping folds.

4. Place in single layer on large baking sheet. Bake 15 to 18 minutes or until pork is barely pink in center and sweet potato is tender. To serve, place packets on plate and cut open, being careful of steam.

Makes 6 servings

family dinners

tuna noodle bake

dairy-free

- 4 tablespoons dairy-free margarine, divided
- 1 small onion, finely chopped
- 2 cloves garlic, minced
- 2 tablespoons sweet rice flour (mochiko)
- 1½ cups soymilk or other dairy-free milk
- 1 teaspoon Italian seasoning
- ½ teaspoon salt
- ½ teaspoon pepper
- ½ teaspoon dried mustard
- ½ teaspoon dried thyme
- 4 cups cooked gluten-free macaroni, rotini or other small pasta shape
- 2 cans (6 ounces each) tuna, drained and flaked
- 2 cups peas
- ½ cup crushed potato chips

1. Preheat oven to 350°F. Melt 2 tablespoons margarine in small skillet. Add onion and garlic; cook and stir 2 minutes or until softened.

2. Melt remaining 2 tablespoons margarine in medium saucepan over low heat. Whisk in rice flour; cook and stir 2 minutes without browning. Stir in soymilk; bring to a boil. Reduce heat; simmer 2 to 3 minutes or until thickened. Stir in Italian seasoning, salt, pepper, mustard and thyme.

3. Combine pasta, onion mixture, tuna and peas in large bowl. Add sauce and combine. Transfer to shallow baking dish or casserole. Sprinkle with potato chips. Cover; bake 15 minutes. Uncover; bake 10 minutes or until hot and bubbly.

Makes 6 to 8 servings

cowboys in the saddle

dairy-free

2 medium baking potatoes, cut into 8 wedges each
¾ teaspoon salt, divided
½ teaspoon black pepper, divided
2 tablespoons canola oil
1 pound skirt steak
¼ teaspoon dried oregano
   Barbecue sauce, warmed

1. Preheat oven to 400°F. Place potato wedges on baking sheet. Sprinkle with ½ teaspoon salt and ¼ teaspoon pepper. Drizzle with oil. Bake 40 minutes or until golden and tender, turning once.

2. Season steak with remaining ¼ teaspoon salt, ¼ teaspoon pepper and oregano. Broil 4 inches from heat 3 to 4 minutes per side or until desired doneness. Slice steak across the grain into 16 strips.

3. Arrange potato wedges on serving plates; drape slice of steak over each potato. Serve with barbecue sauce. **Makes 4 servings**

variation: If desired, grill the skirt steak over medium-high heat 3 to 5 minutes per side, or cook the steak in a stove-top grill pan over medium-high heat.

tip

Many, but not all, commercially available barbecue sauces are gluten-free. As always, check labels. Or create your own barbecue sauce from tomato sauce or paste, spices, vinegar and a touch of brown sugar.

orange chicken stir-fry over quinoa

dairy-free

½ cup uncooked quinoa
1 cup water
4 teaspoons vegetable oil, divided
1 pound thin-sliced boneless skinless chicken breasts, cut into strips
1 cup fresh squeezed orange juice (2 to 3 oranges)
1 tablespoon reduced-sodium soy sauce
1 tablespoon cornstarch
½ cup sliced green onion
2 tablespoons grated fresh ginger
1 cup thinly sliced carrots
6 ounces snow peas
¼ teaspoon red pepper flakes (optional)

1. Place quinoa in fine-mesh strainer; rinse under cold running water. Transfer to medium saucepan; add 1 cup water. Bring to a boil. Reduce heat; cover and simmer 12 to 15 minutes or until water is absorbed and quinoa is tender.

2. Meanwhile, heat 2 teaspoons oil in large skillet over medium-high heat. Add chicken; cook and stir 4 to 6 minutes or until cooked through. Remove and keep warm.

3. Stir orange juice and soy sauce into cornstarch in small bowl until smooth; set aside. Heat remaining 2 teaspoons oil in large skillet. Add green onion and ginger; cook and stir 1 to 2 minutes. Add carrots and snow peas; stir-fry 4 to 5 minutes or until carrots are crisp-tender.

4. Return chicken to skillet; stir orange juice mixture and add to skillet. Bring to a boil. Reduce heat; simmer until slightly thickened. Serve over quinoa and sprinkle with red pepper flakes, if desired.

Makes 4 servings

salmon in the wild

 dairy-free

- **1 package (6 ounces) long grain and wild rice mix**
- **1 tablespoon dairy-free stick margarine,
    cut into small pieces**
- **½ cup shredded carrot**
- **2 cups boiling water**
- **1 pound salmon fillets, skin removed**
- **⅓ cup gluten-free teriyaki sauce**
- **1 sliced orange (optional)**

1. Preheat oven to 350°F. Pour rice and contents of seasoning packet into 8-inch square baking dish. Dot rice with small pieces of margarine and top with carrot. Pour boiling water into baking dish.

2. Cut salmon into 8 pieces and arrange on top of rice mixture. Cover dish with foil and bake 20 minutes. Remove foil; bake 5 minutes or until salmon is cooked and rice is tender.

3. Spoon rice and salmon onto serving plates; drizzle salmon with teriyaki sauce. Garnish with orange slices. **Makes 4 servings**

tip

Teriyaki sauce is made from soy sauce, sugar or honey, spices and vinegar or sake. To find a gluten-free teriyaki sauce, look for a product made with tamari, the Japanese version of soy sauce, which is usually wheat free. Gluten-free teriyaki sauce can also be ordered online.

tropical chicken wings

 dairy-free

1 jar (12 ounces) pineapple preserves
½ cup gluten-free soy sauce
½ cup chopped green onions
3 tablespoons lime juice
2 tablespoons pomegranate molasses or honey
1 tablespoon minced garlic
2 teaspoons sriracha sauce*
¼ teaspoon ground allspice
3 pounds chicken wings, tips removed and split at joints
1 tablespoon toasted sesame seeds

*Sriracha is a spicy chili sauce used as a condiment in Asian cuisines. It can be found in the ethnic section of large supermarkets. Hot pepper sauce may be substituted.

slow cooker directions

1. Combine all ingredients except chicken wings and sesame seeds in slow cooker. Stir well to combine.

2. Add chicken wings to sauce and stir to coat. Cover and cook on LOW 3 to 4 hours or until wings are fork tender.

3. Sprinkle with sesame seeds just before serving.

Makes 6 to 8 servings

family-style frankfurters with rice & red beans

dairy-free

1 tablespoon vegetable oil
1 onion, chopped
½ green bell pepper, chopped
2 cloves garlic, minced
1 can (about 15 ounces) red kidney beans, rinsed and drained
1 can (about 15 ounces) Great Northern beans, rinsed and drained
½ pound gluten-free frankfurters, sliced
1 cup uncooked instant brown rice
1 cup vegetable broth
¼ cup packed brown sugar
¼ cup ketchup
3 tablespoons dark molasses
1 tablespoon Dijon mustard

1. Preheat oven to 350°F. Spray 13×9-inch baking dish with nonstick cooking spray.

2. Heat oil in Dutch oven over medium-high heat. Add onion, bell pepper and garlic; cook and stir 2 minutes or until tender.

3. Add beans, frankfurters, rice, broth, brown sugar, ketchup, molasses and mustard; stir to blend. Transfer to prepared baking dish.

4. Cover tightly with foil; bake 30 minutes or until rice is tender.

Makes 6 servings

sweet and sour chicken

dairy-free

2 tablespoons unseasoned rice vinegar
2 tablespoons gluten-free soy sauce
3 cloves garlic, minced
½ teaspoon minced fresh ginger
¼ teaspoon red pepper flakes (optional)
6 ounces boneless skinless chicken breasts
1 teaspoon vegetable oil
3 green onions, cut into 1-inch pieces
1 large green bell pepper, cut into 1-inch pieces
1 tablespoon cornstarch
½ cup reduced-sodium chicken broth
2 tablespoons apricot fruit spread
1 can (11 ounces) mandarin orange segments, drained
2 cups hot cooked white rice or Chinese egg noodles

1. Combine vinegar, soy sauce, garlic, ginger and red pepper flakes, if desired, in medium bowl. Cut chicken into ½-inch strips; toss with vinegar mixture. Marinate 20 minutes at room temperature.

2. Heat oil in wok or large nonstick skillet over medium heat. Drain chicken; reserve marinade. Add chicken to wok; stir-fry 3 minutes. Stir in green onions and bell pepper.

3. Stir cornstarch into reserved marinade in small bowl until smooth. Add broth, fruit spread and marinade mixture to wok. Cook and stir until chicken is cooked through and sauce is thickened. Add orange segments; stir until heated through. Serve over rice. **Makes 4 servings**

cousin arlene's spaghetti lasagna

8 ounces uncooked gluten-free spaghetti
1 tablespoon butter
1 clove garlic, minced
2 pounds ground beef
1 teaspoon sugar
   Salt and black pepper
2 cans (8 ounces each) tomato sauce
1 can (6 ounces) tomato paste
1 cup (8 ounces) sour cream
3 ounces cream cheese, softened
6 green onions, chopped
¼ cup grated Parmesan cheese

1. Preheat oven to 350°F. Cook and drain spaghetti according to package directions.

2. Meanwhile, melt butter in large skillet over medium heat. Add garlic; cook and stir 1 minute. Add ground beef, sugar, salt and pepper; cook 6 to 8 minutes or until meat is browned, stirring to break up meat. Drain fat. Add tomato sauce and tomato paste; simmer 20 minutes, stirring occasionally.

3. Meanwhile, beat sour cream and cream cheese in medium bowl until smooth. Stir in green onions.

4. Spread ½ cup meat sauce in 2-quart casserole. Layer with half of spaghetti, half of sour cream mixture and half of remaining meat sauce. Repeat layers. Sprinkle with Parmesan cheese. Bake 35 minutes or until heated through.   **Makes 6 servings**

tip: This casserole can be frozen. Thaw it in the refrigerator overnight, then let it come to room temperature before baking. Bake until it is heated through. This recipe can also be doubled to make great leftovers.

better-than-take-out fried rice

 dairy-free

3 tablespoons gluten-free soy sauce
1 tablespoon unseasoned rice vinegar
⅛ teaspoon red pepper flakes
1 red bell pepper
1 tablespoon peanut or vegetable oil
6 green onions, cut into 1-inch pieces
1 tablespoon grated fresh ginger
1½ teaspoons minced garlic
½ pound boneless pork loin or tenderloin, cut into 1-inch pieces
2 cups shredded coleslaw mix
1 package (about 8 ounces) cooked whole grain brown rice

1. Combine soy sauce, vinegar and red pepper flakes in small bowl.

2. Cut bell pepper into 1-inch pieces or into decorative shapes using small cookie cutter.

3. Heat oil in large nonstick skillet or wok over medium-high heat. Add bell pepper, green onions, ginger and garlic; stir-fry 1 minute. Add pork; stir-fry 2 to 3 minutes or until pork is cooked through.

4. Stir in coleslaw mix, rice and soy sauce mixture; cook and stir 1 minute or until heated through.

Makes 4 servings

fish and "chips"

 dairy-free

3 cups gluten-free crisp rice cereal, divided
1 egg
1 tablespoon water
1 pound cod, haddock or other firm white fish fillets
1½ teaspoons Italian seasoning, divided
   Salt and black pepper
2 tablespoons dairy-free margarine, melted
2 medium zucchini, cut into sticks
1 package (8 ounces) carrot sticks
1 tablespoon olive oil

1. Preheat oven to 350°F. Spray large baking sheet with nonstick cooking spray or line with foil. Place 2 cups cereal in resealable food storage bag; coarsely crush. Combine with remaining 1 cup cereal in large shallow dish. Beat egg and water in another shallow dish.

2. Cut fish into 3×2-inch pieces. Sprinkle with 1 teaspoon Italian seasoning. Season with salt and pepper. Dip into egg, turning to coat all sides. Dip in cereal, turning to coat all sides. Place on prepared baking sheet. Drizzle with margarine.

3. Place zucchini and carrot sticks on same baking sheet in single layer. Drizzle with oil and sprinkle with remaining ½ teaspoon Italian seasoning. Season with salt and pepper.

4. Bake 20 to 25 minutes or until fish is opaque in center and vegetables are tender.   **Makes 4 servings**

mexican-style shredded beef

 dairy-free

- **1 boneless beef chuck shoulder roast (about 3 pounds)**
- **1 tablespoon ground cumin**
- **1 tablespoon ground coriander**
- **1 tablespoon chili powder**
- **1 teaspoon salt**
- **½ teaspoon ground red pepper**
- **1 cup salsa or picante sauce**
- **2 tablespoons water**
- **1 tablespoon cornstarch**
- **Taco shells and/or corn tortillas**
- **Shredded dairy-free cheese alternative**

slow cooker directions

1. Cut roast in half. Combine cumin, coriander, chili powder, salt and red pepper in small bowl. Rub over roast. Place ¼ cup salsa in 4-quart slow cooker; top with one piece of beef. Layer ¼ cup salsa, remaining beef and ½ cup salsa in slow cooker. Cover; cook on LOW 8 to 10 hours.

2. Remove roast from cooking liquid; cool slightly. Trim and discard fat. Shred meat with two forks.

3. Let cooking liquid stand 5 minutes to allow fat to rise. Skim off fat. *Turn heat to HIGH.* Blend water and cornstarch in small bowl until smooth. Whisk into liquid in slow cooker. Cook, uncovered, 15 minutes or until thickened.

4. Return beef to slow cooker. Cover; cook 15 minutes or until heated through. Adjust seasonings. Serve in taco shells; sprinkle with dairy-free cheese alternative. Leftover beef may be refrigerated up to 3 days or frozen up to 3 months. **Makes 4 to 6 servings**

shrimp bowls

 dairy-free

1 cup plus 2 tablespoons water
¾ cup short-grain white rice
¼ teaspoon salt
1 tablespoon vegetable oil
2 cups frozen stir-fry vegetables
1 package (12 ounces) cooked baby shrimp, thawed and drained
⅓ to ½ cup gluten-free sweet-and-sour sauce
1 tablespoon gluten-free soy sauce

1. Combine water, rice and salt in small saucepan. Bring to a boil. Reduce heat to low; cover and cook 15 minutes or until rice is tender and liquid is absorbed. Keep warm.

2. Heat vegetable oil in large skillet over medium-high heat. Add vegetables; stir-fry 3 minutes or until crisp-tender. Stir in shrimp. Combine sweet-and-sour sauce and soy sauce in small bowl. Pour over shrimp mixture; heat through.

3. To serve, mound rice onto 4 plates. Make well in center. Spoon shrimp mixture into "bowls." **Makes 4 servings**

tip

If you have trouble finding gluten-free sweet and sour sauce, make your own. Combine ½ cup of pineapple juice with ¼ cup each of brown sugar and cider vinegar and 2 tablespoons of ketchup.

chicken with spinach & celery hash

dairy-free

1 package (16 ounces) refrigerated precooked hash brown potatoes
1 package (8 ounces) celery, thinly sliced
3 teaspoons olive oil, divided
12 chicken tenders (about 1 pound)
½ teaspoon dried thyme
   Salt and black pepper
2 packages (5 ounces each) baby spinach
¼ cup water

1. Combine potatoes and celery in medium bowl.

2. Heat 1½ teaspoons oil in large nonstick skillet over medium-high heat. Add potato mixture; cook about 10 minutes, stirring and turning occasionally until mixture begins to brown. Reduce heat; cook 10 minutes or until mixture is browned.

3. Meanwhile, heat remaining 1½ teaspoons oil in another large nonstick skillet over medium-high heat. Add chicken and thyme; season with salt and pepper. Cook about 5 minutes or until cooked through, turning once. Remove from skillet; keep warm.

4. Add spinach and water to same skillet. Cover; cook about 3 minutes or until spinach wilts, stirring once.

5. Serve spinach and hash brown mixture topped with chicken.

Makes 4 servings

peanutty crispy dessert cups

⅓ cup creamy peanut butter
2 tablespoons butter
3 cups large marshmallows (5 ounces)
3 cups gluten-free chocolate-flavored crisp rice cereal
  Ice cream or frozen yogurt
  Chocolate sauce, colored candies and sprinkles, chopped peanuts,
    strawberries and/or maraschino cherries

1. Heat peanut butter and butter in large saucepan over low heat until melted and smooth. Add marshmallows; cook until melted, stirring constantly. Remove pan from heat; stir in cereal until well blended and cooled slightly.

2. Scoop mixture evenly into 12 standard (2½-inch) nonstick muffin cups; press into bottoms and up sides of cups.

3. Refrigerate 5 to 10 minutes or until set. Remove cups from pan; fill with ice cream and sprinkle with desired toppings. **Makes 12 servings**

valentine almond cookies

 dairy-free

¼ cup (½ stick) dairy-free margarine
⅓ cup sugar
1 egg
1½ cups blanched almond flour
¼ cup sweet rice flour (mochiko)
½ teaspoon baking powder
½ teaspoon salt
½ teaspoon cinnamon
    Cherry Pink Glaze (recipe follows)
    Red or pink sugar or sprinkles

1. Beat margarine and sugar in large bowl with electric mixer until creamy. Add egg; beat until fluffy.

2. Beat in almond flour, sweet rice flour, baking powder, salt and cinnamon. Dough will be soft and somewhat sticky. (If dough is too sticky, beat in additional sweet rice flour by teaspoonfuls.) Shape dough into disc; wrap in plastic and refrigerate at least 1 hour.

3. Divide dough in half. Roll out each half between sheets of waxed paper until ¼ inch thick. Return to refrigerator for 30 minutes.

4. Preheat oven to 350°F. Line baking sheets with parchment paper. Remove top sheet of waxed paper; cut out cookies with heart-shaped cookie cutters. Transfer to prepared baking sheet. Repeat with second half of dough. Roll scraps together and roll out between sheets of waxed paper. Return to refrigerator for 15 minutes before cutting out additional cookies.

5. Bake 10 to 15 minutes or until beginning to brown around edges. Cool on wire racks. Place racks over parchment or waxed paper. Prepare Cherry Pink Glaze; spread over cookies. Sprinkle with colored sugar and decorate as desired. **Makes about 2 dozen cookies**

cherry pink glaze: Place 4 cups powdered sugar in medium bowl. Add 4 to 6 tablespoons maraschino cherry juice, 1 tablespoon at a time, to make a pourable glaze. (Or use water and 1 or 2 drops of red food coloring if cherry juice is not available.) For a more opaque glaze, substitute soymilk or other dairy-free milk for some of cherry juice. For white icing use all soymilk.

kids' pizzas

 dairy-free

3 cups Gluten-Free Flour Blend for Bread (page 46)
2 packages (¼ ounce each) active dry yeast
2 teaspoons xanthan gum
1 teaspoon salt
1¼ cups warm water
¼ cup extra virgin olive oil
3 egg whites
1 tablespoon honey
1 teaspoon cider vinegar

toppings

1 can (about 14 ounces) pizza sauce
Italian seasoning
1 package (about 3 ounces) sliced pepperoni
Shredded dairy-free cheese alternative (optional)

1. Preheat oven to 450°F. Line baking sheets or pizza pans with parchment paper.

2. Mix flour blend, yeast, xanthan gum and salt in large bowl. Whisk 1 cup warm water, oil, egg whites, honey and vinegar in medium bowl. Beat wet ingredients into dry ingredients with electric mixer at low speed until combined. Add additional water by tablespoonfuls until batter is smooth and thick. Beat 5 minutes on medium-high, scraping bowl occasionally.

3. Transfer one sixth of dough to prepared pan. Spread dough into 5- or 6-inch circle using dampened fingers or back of oiled spoon, making crust thicker around edge to hold toppings. Repeat with remaining dough.

4. Bake 8 to 12 minutes or until crust is lightly browned.* Top crusts with pizza sauce, Italian seasoning, pepperoni and cheese alternative, if desired. Bake 2 to 5 minutes or until cheese melts.   **Makes 6 pizzas**

*To freeze pizza crusts for later use, allow them to cool, wrap well and store in the freezer for up to 3 months.

choco-berry cake

dairy-free

**2 cups Gluten-Free All-Purpose Flour Blend, plus
extra for pans (page 9)**
1 cup unsweetened cocoa powder
1 cup granulated sugar
1 cup packed brown sugar
2 teaspoons baking powder
1 teaspoon baking soda
1 teaspoon xanthan gum
1 teaspoon espresso powder (optional)
½ teaspoon salt
1½ cups soymilk or other dairy-free milk
½ cup vegetable oil
2 eggs
2 teaspoons vanilla
1 cup dairy-free semisweet chocolate chips
Fluffy White Frosting (page 82)
1 pint strawberries, sliced (about 2 cups)
Strawberries for garnish

1. Preheat oven to 350°F. Grease and flour two 9-inch round cake pans.

2. Combine flour blend, cocoa, granulated sugar, brown sugar, baking powder, baking soda, xanthan gum, espresso powder, if desired, and salt in large bowl. Mix until well combined.

3. Mix soymilk, oil, eggs and vanilla in medium bowl. Add to dry ingredients; stir until well blended. Stir in chocolate chips.

4. Divide batter between prepared pans. Bake 35 to 45 minutes on center rack of oven until toothpick inserted into center comes out clean.

5. Cool in pans 5 minutes on wire rack; remove from pans and cool completely. Prepare Fluffy White Frosting.

6. Place one layer on serving plate. Spread with thin layer of frosting. Arrange sliced strawberries over frosting. Top with second layer. Frost top and side of cake. Decorate with additional strawberries.

Makes 10 servings

fluffy white frosting

 dairy-free

1½ cups (3 sticks) dairy-free margarine
1½ teaspoons vanilla
6 cups powdered sugar, sifted
½ teaspoon salt
6 tablespoons vanilla-flavor soy coffee creamer

1. Beat margarine and vanilla in medium bowl until light and fluffy.
Add 3 cups powdered sugar and salt; beat until well blended. Add
3 tablespoons creamer; beat until well blended.

2. Gradually add remaining powdered sugar, beating at low speed. Add
additional creamer as needed to make frosting spreadable.

Makes frosting for 2-layer cake

tea party rice pudding

3½ cups milk
⅔ cup quick-cooking rice
1 package (4-serving size) vanilla cook-and-serve pudding and pie
filling mix
¼ cup sugar
¼ teaspoon ground cinnamon
¼ cup dried cherries or cranberries
¼ teaspoon vanilla
Additional ground cinnamon (optional)

1. Combine milk, rice, pudding mix, sugar and cinnamon in medium
saucepan. Bring to a boil over medium heat, stirring occasionally. Cook
and stir about 6 minutes or until thickened.

2. Remove from heat; stir in cherries and vanilla. Cool 5 minutes; spoon
into 6 (6- to 8-ounce) tea cups. Serve warm, or press plastic wrap on the
surface of pudding and refrigerate 1 to 2 hours to serve cold. Sprinkle with
additional cinnamon before serving, if desired. **Makes 6 servings**

almond crescents

   1 cup (2 sticks) butter, softened
   ⅓ cup granulated sugar
   1¾ cups Gluten-Free All-Purpose Flour Blend (page 9)
   ¼ cup cornstarch
   1 teaspoon vanilla
   ½ teaspoon xanthan gum
   1½ cups ground toasted almonds*
   Chocolate Glaze (recipe follows) or powdered sugar

*To toast almonds, spread in single layer on baking sheet. Bake in preheated 350°F oven 8 to 10 minutes or until golden brown, stirring frequently.

1. Preheat oven to 325°F. Beat butter and granulated sugar in large bowl until creamy. Mix in flour blend, cornstarch, vanilla and xanthan gum. Stir in ground almonds. Shape tablespoonfuls of dough into crescents. Place 2 inches apart on ungreased cookie sheets.

2. Bake 22 to 25 minutes or until light brown. Cool 1 minute. Remove to wire racks; cool completely. Prepare Chocolate Glaze; drizzle over cookies. Let stand until set; store in airtight container. Or sprinkle with powdered sugar before serving.   **Makes about 3 dozen cookies**

chocolate glaze: Place ½ cup semisweet chocolate chips and 1 tablespoon butter in small resealable plastic bag. Place bag in bowl of hot water for 2 to 3 minutes or until chocolate is softened. Knead until chocolate mixture is smooth. Cut off very tiny corner of bag. Drizzle chocolate mixture over cookies.

tip

To grind almonds, place them in a food processor or blender. Process the almonds using on/off pulsing action until they are finely ground. Do not overprocess the nuts or you will end up with almond butter. Adding a tablespoon or two of powdered sugar to the almonds before processing can help prevent this.

cherry pink cupcakes

 dairy-free

1 jar (6 ounces) maraschino cherries
1 cup granulated sugar
2 eggs
1¼ cups Gluten-Free All-Purpose Flour Blend (recipe page 9)
1½ teaspoons baking powder
½ teaspoon salt
½ teaspoon xanthan gum
½ cup vegetable oil
½ cup soymilk or other dairy-free milk
1 teaspoon vanilla
Cherry Pink Frosting (recipe follows)
Stemmed cherries (optional)

1. Preheat oven to 350°F. Line 12 standard (2½-inch) muffin cups with paper baking cups. Drain cherries, reserving juice for Cherry Pink Frosting. Chop cherries and squeeze out excess moisture. Spread cherries on paper towels to drain. Set aside.

2. Beat sugar and eggs in large bowl with electric mixer at medium speed until light and fluffy. Combine flour blend, baking powder, salt and xanthan gum in medium bowl. Add dry ingredients to sugar mixture; beat until combined.

3. Add oil, soymilk and vanilla. Beat 1 minute or until smooth. Stir in chopped cherries. Pour batter into prepared muffin cups, filling three-fourths full.

4. Bake 20 minutes or until lightly browned and centers of muffins spring back when gently touched. Cool in pan on wire rack 5 minutes. Remove from pans to wire rack; cool completely. Prepare Cherry Pink Frosting; frost cupcakes and garnish with cherries.   **Makes 12 cupcakes**

cherry pink frosting: Beat ½ cup (1 stick) dairy-free margarine in medium bowl until light and fluffy. Add 1 cup powdered sugar; beat until blended. Add 4 teaspoons of reserved cherry juice and 1 cup powdered sugar. Beat until smooth. Add 1 or 2 drops of red food coloring for a darker color. Add additional powdered sugar until frosting is spreadable.

holiday cut-out cookies dairy-free

¾ cup granulated sugar
½ cup shortening
1 egg
2 cups Gluten-Free All-Purpose Flour Blend (page 9)
½ teaspoon salt
½ teaspoon baking powder
1 teaspoon xanthan gum
1 teaspoon cinnamon
2 teaspoons vanilla
2 tablespoons soymilk or other dairy-free milk
Fluffy White Frosting (optional, page 82)
Food coloring (optional)
Colored sugar

1. Beat granulated sugar and shortening in large bowl with electric mixer 2 minutes or until light and fluffy. Beat in egg.

2. Whisk flour blend, salt, baking powder, xanthan gum and cinnamon in medium bowl. Gradually beat into sugar mixture. Beat in vanilla and 2 tablespoons soymilk to make soft dough. (Add additional milk by teaspoonfuls if dough is too dry.) Divide dough in half; pat into discs. Wrap in plastic and refrigerate 15 minutes.

3. Preheat oven to 350°F. Line baking sheets with parchment paper.

4. Roll out each half of dough between sheets of waxed paper until ¼ inch thick. Cut out cookies and sprinkle with colored sugar, if desired. Transfer to prepared baking sheets. Bake 8 to 10 minutes or until edges begin to brown. Cool completely on wire racks. If desired, prepare Fluffy White Frosting and tint with food coloring. Frost cookies and sprinkle with colored sugar.

Makes about 2 dozen cookies

allergy-free birthday cake

dairy-free

3 cups Gluten-Free All-Purpose Flour Blend, plus extra for
    pans (page 9)
2 cups sugar
6 tablespoons unsweetened cocoa powder
2 teaspoons baking soda
2 teaspoons xanthan gum
1 teaspoon salt
2 cups chocolate soymilk
½ cup plus 2 tablespoons vegetable oil
2 tablespoons cider vinegar
1 teaspoon vanilla
    Chocolate No-Butter Buttercream Frosting (recipe follows)

1. Preheat oven to 350°F. Grease and flour two 9-inch round cake pans.

2. Whisk flour blend, sugar, cocoa, baking soda, xanthan gum and salt in large bowl. Combine soymilk, oil, vinegar and vanilla in small bowl.

3. Pour wet ingredients into dry; stir until smooth, scraping bottom and side of bowl. Immediately pour into prepared pans and place in oven.

4. Bake 25 to 30 minutes or until toothpick inserted into centers comes out clean. Cool in pans 5 minutes. Carefully invert onto wire rack; cool completely.

5. Prepare Chocolate No-Butter Buttercream Frosting. Frost cake. Decorate as desired.

Makes 10 servings

chocolate no-butter buttercream frosting: Beat ½ cup (1 stick) dairy-free margarine (not spread) with electric mixer at medium speed until light and fluffy. Add 2 teaspoons vanilla. Gradually beat in ½ cup unsweetened cocoa powder and 3½ cups powdered sugar. Add 4 to 6 tablespoons soy creamer 1 tablespoon at a time until spreadable.

orange snickerdoodles

 dairy-free

½ cup (1 stick) dairy-free margarine
1 cup granulated sugar
1 tablespoon grated orange peel
1 egg
½ teaspoon vanilla
1½ cups Gluten-Free All-Purpose Flour Blend (page 9)
¾ teaspoon xanthan gum
½ teaspoon baking soda
½ teaspoon cream of tartar
¼ cup orange-colored sugar*

icing

1 cup powdered sugar
2 tablespoons orange juice
¼ teaspoon vanilla

Or substitute granulated sugar.

1. Beat margarine in large bowl with electric mixer at medium speed 30 seconds. Add granulated sugar and orange peel; beat 1 minute. Beat in egg and vanilla until well blended. Add flour blend, xanthan gum, baking soda and cream of tartar; beat until just combined. Cover with plastic wrap; refrigerate 1 hour.

2. Preheat oven to 375°F. Line cookie sheets with parchment paper.

3. Shape dough into 1-inch balls; roll in orange-colored sugar. Place balls 2 inches apart on prepared cookie sheets. Bake 12 to 15 minutes or until edges are light brown. Cool on cookie sheets 5 minutes.

4. Meanwhile, for icing, whisk powdered sugar, orange juice and vanilla in small bowl until sugar is dissolved. Add more powdered sugar or juice to reach desired consistency.

5. Gently loosen cookies from parchment, but leave on sheets. Drizzle icing evenly over warm cookies using a whisk or fork. Transfer to wire racks; cool completely. Icing will firm as cookies cool. Store in airtight container. **Makes about 3 dozen cookies**

easy holiday shortbread cookies

1 cup (2 sticks) unsalted butter, softened
½ cup powdered sugar
2 tablespoons packed light brown sugar
¼ teaspoon salt
1½ cups Gluten-Free All-Purpose Flour Blend (page 9)
½ cup sweet rice flour (mochiko)
1 teaspoon xanthan gum

1. Beat butter, powdered sugar, brown sugar and salt in large bowl with electric mixer at medium speed 2 minutes or until light and fluffy. Whisk flour blend, sweet rice flour and xanthan gum in medium bowl.

2. Add flour mixture to butter mixture, ½ cup at a time, beating well after each addition. Shape dough into 14-inch-long log. Wrap tightly in plastic wrap; refrigerate 1 hour.*

3. Preheat oven to 300°F. Cut log into ½-inch-thick slices; place on ungreased cookie sheets.

4. Bake about 25 minutes or until lightly browned. Cool 5 minutes on cookie sheets; remove to wire racks to cool completely.

Makes about 2 dozen cookies

*Dough can be stored in the refrigerator up to two days, or in the freezer for up to one month. If frozen, thaw the dough log in the refrigerator overnight before slicing and baking.

tip

Sweet rice flour is different from regular rice flour. It is an excellent thickener and a good ingredient to know for gluten-free baking. Sweet rice flour is made from short grain "sticky" rice, the kind often used in Asian desserts. The Japanese term for this flour is mochiko since it is used in making mochi (rice cakes). Look for it in the Asian section of large supermarkets or order it online.

raspberry crispy hearts

¼ cup (½ stick) butter
1 package (10½ ounces) miniature marshmallows
⅛ teaspoon salt
½ cup seedless raspberry jam
   Pink or red food coloring (optional)
6 cups gluten-free crisp rice cereal
2 cups chocolate chips, melted

1. Spray 13×9-inch baking pan with nonstick cooking spray. Melt butter in large saucepan over medium heat. Add marshmallows and salt; cook and stir until mixture is melted and smooth.

2. Stir in jam until well blended. Add food coloring, if desired, a few drops at a time, until desired shade of pink is reached. Stir in cereal until completely blended.

3. Immediately scoop mixture into prepared pan; spread into even layer with dampened hands. (Mixture will be very sticky.) Let stand about 1 hour or until completely cool, or refrigerate to speed up cooling.

4. Remove bars from pan to cutting board. Spray 3-inch heart-shaped cookie cutter with nonstick cooking spray; cut out hearts from bars.

5. Spread melted chocolate over each heart; use toothpick to create swirls in chocolate.

Makes about 2 dozen hearts

tip: These cookies are best eaten the day they are made.

mr. froggy

dairy-free

1 avocado
Salt and pepper
Juice of 1 lime
4 ounces deli ham or turkey
4 corn tortillas
Grape tomatoes

1. Mash avocado in small bowl; season with salt and pepper. Stir in lime juice. Keep covered. Cut out 4 tongue shapes from 1 slice of ham; shred remaining ham.

2. Working with one tortilla at a time, microwave tortilla on HIGH 20 to 30 seconds to soften. Fold tortilla in half; cut long ovals for eyes being careful to leave bottom edge of eye intact. Spread half of tortilla with avocado and top with shredded ham. Fold over, leaving eyes sticking up.

3. Heat large nonstick skillet over medium-high heat. Cook tortillas 1 to 2 minutes per side until heated through and lightly browned. Place on serving plate and add ham tongues and tomato slices for eyes.

Makes 4 servings

carrot-spice snack cake
 dairy-free

½ cup packed brown sugar
⅓ cup dairy-free margarine
2 eggs
½ cup soymilk or other dairy-free milk
1 teaspoon vanilla
1¼ cups Gluten-Free All-Purpose Flour Blend (page 9)
¾ cup finely shredded carrot
2 teaspoons baking powder
1½ teaspoons pumpkin pie spice
½ teaspoon xanthan gum
½ teaspoon salt
⅓ cup golden raisins
Powdered sugar

1. Preheat oven to 350°F. Spray 8-inch square baking pan with nonstick cooking spray.

2. Beat sugar and margarine in medium bowl with electric mixer at medium speed until well blended. Beat in eggs, soymilk and vanilla.

3. Stir in flour blend, carrot, baking powder, pumpkin pie spice, xanthan gum and salt. Stir in raisins.

4. Spread batter in prepared pan. Bake 25 to 30 minutes or until toothpick inserted into center comes out clean. Cool completely in pan on wire rack. Just before serving, sprinkle with powdered sugar.   **Makes 8 servings**

banana & chocolate chip pops

1 small ripe banana
1 carton (6 ounces) banana yogurt
⅛ teaspoon ground nutmeg
2 tablespoons mini chocolate chips
Pop molds or paper cups

1. Slice banana; place in food processor with yogurt and nutmeg. Process until smooth. Transfer to small bowl; stir in chips.

2. Spoon banana mixture into 4 plastic pop molds. Place tops on molds; set in provided stand. Set on level surface in freezer; freeze 2 hours or until firm. To unmold, briefly run warm water over pop molds until each pop loosens. *Makes 4 servings*

peanut butter & jelly pops: Stir ¼ cup peanut butter in small bowl until smooth; stir in 1 carton vanilla yogurt. Drop 2 tablespoons strawberry fruit spread on top of mixture; pull spoon back and forth through mixture several times to swirl slightly. Spoon into 4 molds and freeze as directed above. Makes 4 servings.

blueberry-lime pops: Stir 1 carton key lime yogurt in small bowl until smooth; fold in ⅓ cup frozen blueberries. Spoon into 4 molds and freeze as directed above. Makes 4 servings.

tip

You can also make pops in paper cups instead of pop molds. Use small (5- to 7- ounce paper cups and fill them two-thirds full with the pop mixture. After 20 to 30 minutes, insert a wooden pop stick into each cup. Freeze at least 2 hours or until firm.

mini beef tostadas

1 pound ground beef
1 tablespoon instant minced onion
1 can (8 ounces) refried beans
1 can (4 ounces) chopped green chiles, drained (optional)
½ cup gluten-free taco sauce
4 dozen round corn tortilla chips
1 cup (4 ounces) shredded Cheddar cheese

1. Preheat oven to 375°F. Brown beef and onion in large skillet over medium heat 6 to 8 minutes; drain fat.

2. Stir in beans, chiles, if desired, and taco sauce; cook and stir about 4 minutes or until bubbly. Spoon about 1 heaping tablespoon beef mixture on each tortilla chip; sprinkle with cheese. Place on baking sheets.

3. Bake 2 minutes or until cheese is melted. **Makes 4 dozen tostadas**

dairy-free variation: Omit cheese or replace with a dairy-free cheese alternative.

cherry tomato pops

4 part-skim mozzarella string cheese sticks (1 ounce each)
8 cherry tomatoes
3 tablespoons gluten-free ranch dressing

1. Slice cheese sticks in half lengthwise. Trim stem end of each cherry tomato and remove pulp and seeds.

2. Press end of cheese stick into hollowed tomato to make cherry tomato pop. Serve with ranch dressing for dipping. **Makes 8 pops**

snake snacks

 dairy-free

2 small ripe bananas
1 tablespoon fresh lemon juice
10 to 12 medium strawberries
Poppy seeds (optional)

1. Cut bananas crosswise into ¼-inch slices. Place in medium bowl; toss gently with lemon juice to prevent bananas from turning brown.

2. Leave 2 medium strawberries whole; cut remaining medium strawberries crosswise into ¼-inch slices.

3. Place whole strawberries on serving plates for heads; alternate banana and strawberry slices behind heads to form snakes.

4. Cut 4 small pieces of banana for eyes; arrange on snake heads. Place poppy seed in center of each eye, if desired. Make tongues with slivers of strawberry.

Makes 2 servings

tip: Try to choose strawberries that are about the same diameter as the banana so all the fruit slices that make up the snake will be close to the same width.

Bananas are one of the few fruits that continues to ripen after being picked. To speed up the process, place unripe bananas in a loosely closed brown paper bag at room temperature. Perfectly ripe bananas may be kept that way in the refrigerator for a few days. The skins will darken, but the flesh will stay the same.

gf graham crackers

dairy-free

½ cup sweet rice flour (mochiko), plus additional
    for rolling dough
⅓ cup tapioca flour
½ cup sorghum flour
½ cup lightly packed brown sugar
½ teaspoon baking soda
½ teaspoon salt
¼ cup (½ stick) dairy-free margarine
2 tablespoons plus 2 teaspoons soymilk or other dairy-free milk
2 tablespoons honey
1 tablespoon vanilla

1. Combine sweet rice flour, tapioca flour, sorghum flour, brown sugar, baking soda and salt in bowl of food processor. Pulse to combine, making sure brown sugar is free of lumps. Add margarine and pulse until coarse crumbs form.

2. Stir together soymilk, honey and vanilla in measuring cup until honey dissolves. Pour into flour mixture and process until dough comes together. Dough will be very soft and sticky. Transfer dough to rice-floured surface; pat into rectangle. Wrap dough in plastic and refrigerate at least 4 hours or up to 2 days.

3. Preheat oven to 325°F. Cover work surface with parchment paper and generously flour parchment paper with rice flour.

4. Roll dough to ⅛-inch thick rectangle on parchment using floured rolling pin. If dough becomes too sticky, return to refrigerator or freezer for several minutes. Transfer dough on parchment paper to baking sheet. Score dough into cracker shapes (do not cut all the way through.) Prick dough in rows with tines of fork. Place baking sheet in freezer for 5 to 10 minutes or in refrigerator for 15 to 20 minutes.

5. Transfer cold crackers directly to oven; bake 25 minutes or until firm and a shade darker. Slide parchment onto wire rack to cool. Cut crackers apart when cooled slightly.   **Makes about 1 dozen crackers**

s'mores: Place chocolate squares on GF Graham Crackers. Top with toasted marshmallows and additional GF Graham Crackers.

polenta pizzas

1 teaspoon olive oil
½ cup chopped onion
¼ pound bulk mild Italian sausage
1 can (8 ounces) pizza sauce
1 roll (16 ounces) prepared polenta
1 cup (4 ounces) shredded mozzarella cheese

1. Preheat oven to 350°F. Spray 13×9-inch baking pan with nonstick cooking spray.

2. Heat oil in large skillet over medium heat. Add onion; cook and stir 3 minutes or until tender. Add sausage; brown 5 minutes, stirring to break up meat. Stir in pizza sauce; simmer 5 minutes.

3. Cut polenta roll into 16 slices; arrange in prepared pan. Spoon 1 heaping tablespoon sausage mixture over each polenta slice. Sprinkle 1 tablespoon cheese over each slice. Bake 15 minutes or until polenta is hot and cheese is melted.

Makes 4 to 6 servings

carrot stix

 dairy-free

1 package (16 ounces) carrots
2 teaspoons olive oil
½ teaspoon salt
¼ teaspoon black pepper
1 teaspoon sugar
¼ teaspoon ground cinnamon

1. Preheat oven to 375°F. Line large baking sheet with foil.

2. Cut carrots in half crosswise. Cut each piece lengthwise into strips. Combine carrot sticks, oil, salt and pepper in large bowl. Toss to coat.

3. Arrange carrots on prepared baking sheet. Bake 20 minutes, turning once.

4. Meanwhile, combine sugar and cinnamon in small bowl.

5. Transfer baked carrots to large bowl. Sprinkle with sugar mixture; toss to coat. Serve immediately.   Makes 4 to 6 servings

note: One bag (16 ounces) of baby carrots can be substituted for the large carrots. Bake for 25 minutes.

taco popcorn olé

 dairy-free

9 cups plain popped popcorn
   Butter-flavored cooking spray
1 teaspoon chili powder
½ teaspoon salt
½ teaspoon garlic powder
⅛ teaspoon ground red pepper (optional)

1. Preheat oven to 350°F. Line 15×10-inch jelly-roll pan with foil.

2. Place popcorn in single layer on prepared pan. Coat lightly with cooking spray.

3. Combine chili powder, salt, garlic powder and red pepper, if desired, in small bowl. Sprinkle spice mixture over popcorn; mix lightly to coat evenly.

4. Bake 5 minutes or until heated through, stirring gently after 3 minutes. Spread popcorn in single layer on large sheet of foil to cool.
     Makes 6 servings

tip: Store popcorn in tightly covered container at room temperature up to 4 days.

 tip

You can easily flavor the popcorn to your family's taste.
For a spicier, smoky version, use a chipotle chili powder.
Or omit the chili powder, garlic powder and red pepper
and use your favorite seasoned salt instead.

triple berry blast

 dairy-free

Coarse sugar
1 cup frozen mixed berries
1 cup soymilk* or other dairy-free milk
½ cup sliced banana
2 teaspoons honey

*Do not use vanilla-flavored soymilk because it will make this smoothie too sweet.

1. Place sugar in small shallow dish. Wet rims of 2 glasses with damp paper towel; dip rims into sugar. Place glasses upright to dry.

2. Combine berries, soymilk, banana and honey in blender. Process about 30 seconds or until fruit is puréed and mixture is smooth.

3. Pour into prepared glasses. Serve immediately.   Makes 2 servings

green meanies

 dairy-free

4 green apples
1 cup nut butter (cashew, almond or peanut butter)
Almond slivers

1. Place apple, stem side up, on cutting board. Cut away 2 halves from sides of apple, leaving 1-inch-thick center slice with stem and core. Discard core slice. Cut each half round in half. Cut each apple quarter into two wedges using a crinkle cutter to create teeth.

2. Spread 2 teaspoons nut butter on wide edge of apple slice. Top with another apple slice, aligning crinkled edges to resemble jaws. Insert almond slivers to make fangs.   Makes 8 servings

mud hole dunk

4 cups fresh berries, oranges or other fruit
1 cup prepared creamy chocolate frosting*
Assorted decorator sprinkles or flaked coconut

*Do not use whipped frosting.

1. Line baking sheet with waxed paper; set aside. Pat fruit dry with paper towels.

2. Place frosting in small bowl; microwave on HIGH 15 to 20 seconds or until melted, stirring once.

3. Dip fruit halfway into frosting, allowing excess to drip off. Roll in desired sprinkles or coconut. Place on prepared baking sheet. Refrigerate about 10 minutes or until frosting is set. *Makes 8 servings*

peachy pops

1 package (16 ounces) frozen sliced peaches, partially thawed
2 containers (6 ounces each) peach or vanilla yogurt
¼ cup honey
12 small paper cups
12 wooden pop sticks
Colored sugar or sugar sprinkles

1. Combine peaches, yogurt and honey in food processor or blender; process about 20 seconds or until smooth.

2. Pour mixture into paper cups, filling two thirds full, and place on baking sheet. Freeze 30 minutes or until mixture begins to harden. Push sticks into centers and freeze 3 hours or until firm.

3. Tear paper away from pops; roll pops in sugar. Serve immediately or return to freezer until ready to serve. *Makes 12 servings*

blt cukes

 dairy-free

½ cup finely chopped lettuce
½ cup finely chopped baby spinach
 3 slices bacon, crisp-cooked and crumbled
¼ cup finely diced tomato
 1 tablespoon plus 1½ teaspoons dairy-free mayonnaise
¼ teaspoon black pepper
⅛ teaspoon salt
 1 large cucumber
   Minced fresh parsley or green onion (optional)

1. Combine lettuce, spinach, bacon, tomato, mayonnaise, pepper and salt in medium bowl; mix well.

2. Peel cucumber; trim off ends and cut in half lengthwise. Use spoon to scoop out seeds; discard seeds.

3. Divide bacon mixture between cucumber halves, mounding in center. Garnish with parsley. Cut into 2-inch pieces.   *Makes 8 to 10 pieces*

tip

Most commercially available mayonnaise is dairy-free. Vegan mayonnaise, made without eggs or dairy, is also available in the refrigerated dairy section of most supermarkets. Those following a vegan diet have eliminated not only meat, fish and poultry, but also all other animal products, including dairy, eggs and honey.

cinnamon caramel corn

8 cups plain popped popcorn
2 tablespoons honey
4 teaspoons butter
¼ teaspoon ground cinnamon

1. Preheat oven to 350°F. Spray jelly-roll pan with nonstick cooking spray. Place popcorn in large bowl.

2. Combine honey, butter and cinnamon in small saucepan; cook and stir over low heat until butter is melted and mixture is smooth. Immediately pour over popcorn; toss to coat evenly. Spread onto prepared pan.

3. Bake 12 to 14 minutes or until coating is golden brown and appears crackled, stirring twice.

4. Cool popcorn on pan. (As popcorn cools, coating becomes crisp. If not crisp enough, or if popcorn softens upon standing, return to oven and heat 5 to 8 minutes.) Store in airtight container.   **Makes 4 servings**

cajun popcorn: Preheat oven and prepare jelly-roll pan as directed above. Replace cinnamon with 1 teaspoon cajun or creole seasoning and add 1 extra teaspoon honey. Proceed with recipe as directed above.

italian popcorn: Spray 8 cups popped popcorn with butter-flavored cooking spray to coat. Sprinkle with 2 tablespoons grated parmesan cheese, ½ teaspoon dried oregano and ⅛ teaspoon black pepper. Gently toss to coat. Bake 5 to 8 minutes or until heated through, stirring once.

sweet sushi

dairy-free

1 package (about 10 ounces) marshmallows
3 tablespoons dairy-free margarine
6 cups gluten-free crisp rice cereal
   Green fruit roll-ups
   Sliced strawberries, peaches and kiwi
   Gummy fish

1. Spray 13×9-inch baking pan with nonstick cooking spray.

2. Place marshmallows and butter in large microwavable bowl; microwave on HIGH 1 to 2 minutes or until melted and smooth, stirring once. Immediately stir in cereal until coated. Press mixture into prepared pan using waxed paper to press into even layer. Let stand 10 minutes.

3. Cut half of cereal treat into 2×1-inch rectangles; round edges of rectangles slightly. Cut remaining half of treat into 1½- to 2-inch circles using greased cookie or biscuit cutter.

4. Cut fruit roll-ups into ½-inch-wide and 1-inch-wide strips. Top rectangles with candy or fruit; wrap with ½-inch fruit roll-up strips as shown in photo. Wrap 1-inch strips around circles; top with fruit or candy.

Makes 3 to 4 dozen pieces

rocky road brownies

½ cup (1 stick) dairy-free margarine
½ cup unsweetened cocoa powder
 1 cup sugar
¼ cup soymilk or other dairy-free milk
 2 eggs
 2 teaspoons vanilla
⅔ cup Gluten-Free All-Purpose Flour Blend (page 9)
½ teaspoon salt
½ teaspoon baking powder
½ teaspoon xanthan gum
 1 cup miniature marshmallows
 1 cup coarsely chopped walnuts
 1 cup (6 ounces) dairy-free semisweet chocolate chips

1. Preheat oven to 350°F. Grease 8-inch square baking pan.

2. Combine margarine and cocoa in large saucepan over low heat, stirring constantly until smooth. Remove from heat; whisk in sugar, soymilk, eggs and vanilla until smooth.

3. Combine flour blend, salt, baking powder and xanthan gum in small bowl. Add to wet ingredients in saucepan; stir until blended. Spread batter evenly in prepared baking pan.

4. Bake 25 to 35 minutes or until center feels dry. Sprinkle with marshmallows, walnuts and chocolate chips. Bake 3 to 5 minutes or until topping is slightly melted. Cool in pan on wire rack.

Makes 16 brownies

sky blue fluffer slusher dairy-free

1 package (4-serving size) berry blue gelatin
1 cup very cold water
2 cups crushed ice
1 jar (7 ounces) marshmallow creme
   Miniature marshmallows and maraschino cherries (optional)

1. Dissolve gelatin in cold water in small bowl.

2. Combine gelatin mixture, crushed ice and marshmallow creme in blender. Blend 30 seconds to 1 minute or until mixture reaches slushy consistency.

3. Pour slushy into chilled glasses; top with miniature marshmallows and a cherry.

Makes 4 servings

jiggly banana split

3 gelatin snack cups (3 ounces each), any flavors
1 banana
3 tablespoons whipped topping
   Colored sprinkles
1 maraschino cherry

1. Unmold snack cups by dipping partially in warm water for a few seconds. Slide gelatin from cups into center of serving dish.

2. Peel banana and cut in half lengthwise. Place banana slices on each side of gelatin.

3. Top with dollops of whipped topping, sprinkles and cherry.

Makes 2 servings

'nana cupcakes

dairy-free

2 cups Gluten-Free All-Purpose Flour Blend (page 9)
1½ cups granulated sugar
2 tablespoons packed brown sugar
2 teaspoons baking powder
¾ teaspoon xanthan gum
½ teaspoon salt
½ teaspoon ground cinnamon
¼ teaspoon ground allspice
½ cup vegetable oil
2 eggs
¼ cup soymilk or other dairy-free milk
1 teaspoon vanilla
2 mashed bananas
Chocolate No-Butter Buttercream Frosting (recipe follows)
Gluten-free chocolate sprinkles (optional)

1. Preheat oven to 350°F. Line 18 standard (2½-inch) muffin cups with paper baking cups.

2. Combine flour blend, granulated sugar, brown sugar, baking powder, xanthan gum, salt, cinnamon and allspice in large bowl. Add oil, eggs, soymilk and vanilla; beat with electric mixer at medium speed 2 minutes or until well blended. Beat in bananas until well blended. Spoon batter into prepared muffin cups, filling three-fourths full.

3. Bake 25 to 30 minutes or until toothpick inserted into centers comes out clean. Cool cupcakes in pans on wire racks 10 minutes. Remove to wire racks; cool completely.

4. Prepare Chocolate No-Butter Buttercream Frosting. Frost cupcakes; decorate with sprinkles, if desired.   **Makes 18 cupcakes**

chocolate no-butter buttercream frosting: Beat ½ cup (1 stick) dairy-free margarine (not spread) with electric mixer at medium speed until light and fluffy. Add 2 teaspoons vanilla. Gradually beat in ½ cup unsweetened cocoa powder and 3½ cups powdered sugar. Add 4 to 6 tablespoons soy creamer 1 tablespoon at a time until spreadable.

perfect peanut butter pudding

  2 cups milk
  2 eggs
  ⅓ cup creamy peanut butter
  ¼ cup packed brown sugar
  ¼ teaspoon vanilla
  ¾ cup shaved gluten-free chocolate or shredded coconut (optional)

1. Preheat oven to 350°F. Grease six 3-ounce ovenproof custard cups.

2. Combine milk, eggs, peanut butter, brown sugar and vanilla in blender; blend at high 1 minute. Pour into prepared custard cups. Place cups in 13×9-inch baking dish; carefully add enough hot water to baking dish to come halfway up sides of custard cups.

3. Bake 50 minutes or until pudding is set. Remove custard cups from pan; cool to room temperature. Refrigerate until serving.

4. Just before serving, top each pudding with shaved chocolate, if desired.

Makes 6 servings

tip

If peanut butter is not an option for your child, make this pudding with another variety of nut butter. Almond butter, cashew butter and macadamia butter are all delicious and widely available. If you need to avoid tree nuts as well, sunflower seed butter is usually a good choice.

"hot" chocolate smoothie

2½ cups chocolate frozen yogurt
1¾ cups chocolate soymilk
1 banana
⅛ teaspoon chipotle chili powder
1½ cups cubed or crushed ice
Chocolate shavings (optional)

Combine frozen yogurt, soymilk, banana, chili powder and ice in blender.
Process until smooth, stopping once to scrape down sides. Pour into
4 glasses. Top with chocolate shavings. Serve immediately.

Makes 4 servings

popcorn truffles

 dairy-free

8 cups plain popped popcorn
2 cups (12 ounces) dairy-free semisweet chocolate chips
Colored sprinkles (optional)

1. Line 2 baking sheets with waxed paper. Place popcorn in large bowl.

2. Place chocolate chips in microwavable bowl. Microwave on HIGH
30 seconds; stir. Repeat, if necessary, until chips are melted. Pour over
popcorn; stir until well coated.

3. Scoop popcorn mixture with small ice cream scoop, pressing mixture
slightly against the inside of bowl. Drop by scoopfuls onto prepared
baking sheets. Decorate with sprinkles, if desired. Allow to harden at room
temperature or refrigerate. Store truffles in airtight container up to 3 days.

Makes about 40 truffles

mexican chocolate macaroons

dairy-free

8 squares (1 ounce each) dairy-free semisweet chocolate, divided
1¾ cups plus ⅓ cup whole almonds, divided
¾ cup sugar
2 egg whites
1 teaspoon ground cinnamon
1 teaspoon vanilla

1. Preheat oven to 400°F. Grease cookie sheets.

2. Coarsely chop 5 squares of chocolate in food processor. Add 1¾ cups almonds and sugar; process using on/off pulsing action until mixture is finely ground. Add egg whites, cinnamon and vanilla; process just until mixture forms moist dough.

3. Shape dough into 1-inch balls. (Dough will be sticky.) Place 2 inches apart on prepared cookie sheets. Press 1 whole almond into center of each dough ball.

4. Bake 8 to 10 minutes or just until set. Cool on cookie sheets 2 minutes. Remove to wire racks; cool completely.

5. Place remaining 3 squares of chocolate in small resealable food storage bag; seal. Microwave on HIGH 1 minute; knead bag. Microwave at additional 30-second intervals until chocolate is melted, kneading after each interval. Cut off small corner of bag. Drizzle chocolate over cookies. Let stand until set. Store in airtight container.

Makes about 3 dozen cookies

chocolate chip peanut butter cookies

 dairy-free

1⅓ cups Gluten-Free All-Purpose Flour Blend (page 9)
½ teaspoon salt
½ teaspoon baking soda
½ teaspoon xanthan gum
½ cup (1 stick) dairy-free margarine
½ cup creamy peanut butter
½ cup granulated sugar
¼ cup packed light brown sugar
1 egg, lightly beaten
1 teaspoon vanilla
1 cup semisweet chocolate chips
½ cup peanuts

1. Preheat oven to 350°F. Lightly grease cookie sheets.

2. Combine flour blend, salt, baking soda and xanthan gum in medium bowl. Beat margarine, peanut butter, granulated sugar and brown sugar in large bowl with electric mixer at medium speed until light and fluffy. Add egg and vanilla; beat until well blended. Add flour mixture; beat just until blended. Stir in chocolate chips and peanuts.

3. Drop dough by rounded tablespoonfuls 2 inches apart onto prepared cookie sheets. Flatten slightly with spatula.

4. Bake 12 to 14 minutes or until edges are lightly browned. Cool 2 minutes on cookie sheets. Remove to wire racks; cool completely.

Makes about 2½ dozen cookies

one-bite pineapple chewies

½ cup whipping cream
¼ cup sugar
⅛ teaspoon salt
1 cup finely chopped dried pineapple
½ cup coarsely chopped slivered almonds
¼ cup mini semisweet chocolate chips
¼ cup white rice flour

1. Preheat oven to 350°F. Line 2 cookie sheets with parchment paper.

2. Stir together cream, sugar and salt in large bowl until sugar dissolves. Stir in pineapple, almonds and chocolate chips. Stir in rice flour until blended.

3. Drop dough by rounded teaspoonfuls about 1 inch apart onto prepared cookie sheets. Bake 13 to 15 minutes or until edges are golden brown. Cool on cookie sheets 2 minutes. Remove to wire racks to cool completely.

Makes about 1½ dozen cookies

chocolate cereal bars

 dairy-free

6 cups gluten-free crisp rice cereal
1 jar (7 ounces) marshmallow creme
1 cup (6 ounces) dairy-free semisweet chocolate chips
2 tablespoons dairy-free margarine
1 teaspoon vanilla

1. Grease 13×9-inch baking pan. Place cereal in large heatproof bowl.

2. Melt marshmallow creme, chocolate chips and margarine in small heavy saucepan over medium heat, stirring occasionally. Remove from heat; stir in vanilla.

3. Pour chocolate mixture over cereal; stir until blended. Press into prepared pan. Cool before cutting into squares.

Makes 24 bars

one-bite pineapple chewies

plum-side down cakes

dairy-free

2 tablespoons dairy-free margarine
3 tablespoons packed light brown sugar
3 plums, sliced
½ cup granulated sugar
2 tablespoons shortening
1 egg
1¼ cups Gluten-Free All-Purpose Flour Blend (page 9)
1½ teaspoons baking powder
½ teaspoon xanthan gum
¼ teaspoon salt
⅓ cup soymilk or other dairy-free milk
½ teaspoon vanilla

1. Preheat oven to 350°F. Spray 8 standard (2½-inch) muffin cups with nonstick cooking spray.

2. Place margarine in small microwavable bowl. Microwave on LOW (30%) just until melted. Stir in brown sugar. Spoon evenly into prepared muffin cups. Pat plum slices dry and arrange in bottom of each cup.

3. Beat granulated sugar and shortening in medium bowl with electric mixer at medium speed until fluffy. Beat in egg until well combined. Combine flour blend, baking powder, xanthan gum and salt in small bowl; beat into shortening mixture. Add soymilk and vanilla; beat 1 minute or until smooth.

4. Spoon batter into prepared muffin cups, filling three-fourths full; smooth tops. Place pan on baking sheet to catch drips. Bake 20 to 22 minutes or until toothpick inserted into centers comes out clean.

5. Cool in pan 10 minutes. Run a knife around each cup. Invert onto wire rack; cool completely.

Makes 8 cupcakes

banana freezer pops

 dairy-free

2 ripe medium bananas
1 can (6 ounces) frozen orange juice concentrate
¼ cup water
1 tablespoon honey
1 teaspoon vanilla
8 (3-ounce) paper or plastic cups
8 wooden pop sticks

1. Peel bananas; break into chunks. Place in food processor or blender.

2. Add orange juice concentrate, water, honey and vanilla; process until smooth.

3. Pour banana mixture evenly into cups, filling three-fourths full. Cover top of each cup with small piece of foil. Insert wooden stick through center of foil into banana mixture.

4. Place cups on tray; freeze about 3 hours or until firm. To serve, remove foil and tear off paper cups (or slide out of plastic cups).

Makes 8 servings

peppy purple pops: Omit honey and vanilla. Substitute grape juice concentrate for orange juice concentrate.

frozen banana shakes: Increase water to 1½ cups. Prepare fruit mixture as directed. Add 4 ice cubes; process on high speed until mixture is thick and creamy. Makes 3 servings.

tip

The vast majority of bananas sold in the U.S. are the Cavendish variety. There are many other kinds of bananas, too. Try cute little dwarf or finger bananas when they are available. They look like baby Cavendish but are a bit sweeter. And just for fun, try peeling bananas from the bottom (non-stem end), which is actually a bit easier. It's how the monkeys do it after all.

sweet potato spice cupcakes

dairy-free

  2 cups mashed sweet potatoes*
1½ cups Gluten-Free All-Purpose Flour Blend (page 9)
1¼ cups granulated sugar
  2 teaspoons baking powder
  1 teaspoon baking soda
  1 teaspoon ground cinnamon
  ½ teaspoon salt
  ½ teaspoon xanthan gum
  ¼ teaspoon ground allspice
  ¾ cup canola oil
  2 eggs
  ½ cup chopped walnuts or pecans, plus additional for garnish
  ½ cup raisins
     Cream Cheese Frosting (recipe follows)

*About 1½ pounds sweet potatoes, cooked, peeled and mashed

1. Preheat oven to 325°F. Line 18 standard (2½-inch) muffin cups with paper baking cups.

2. Whisk flour blend, granulated sugar, baking powder, baking soda, cinnamon, salt, xanthan gum and allspice in medium bowl. Beat mashed sweet potato, oil and eggs in large bowl with electric mixer at low speed until blended. Add flour mixture; beat at medium speed 30 seconds or until well blended. Stir in ½ cup walnuts and raisins. Spoon batter evenly into prepared muffin cups.

3. Bake 25 to 30 minutes or until toothpick inserted into centers comes out clean. Cool in pan on wire rack 10 minutes. Remove from pan. Prepare Cream Cheese Frosting. Frost cupcakes; garnish with walnuts.

Makes 18 cupcakes

cream cheese frosting: Beat 1 package (8 ounces) dairy-free cream cheese alternative and ¼ cup (½ stick) dairy-free margarine (not spread) in medium bowl with electric mixer at medium-high speed until creamy. Gradually beat in 1½ cups sifted powdered sugar until well blended. Beat in ¼ teaspoon salt and ¼ teaspoon vanilla. Makes about 3 cups.

Metric Conversion Chart

VOLUME MEASUREMENTS (dry)

$1/8$ teaspoon = 0.5 mL
$1/4$ teaspoon = 1 mL
$1/2$ teaspoon = 2 mL
$3/4$ teaspoon = 4 mL
1 teaspoon = 5 mL
1 tablespoon = 15 mL
2 tablespoons = 30 mL
$1/4$ cup = 60 mL
$1/3$ cup = 75 mL
$1/2$ cup = 125 mL
$2/3$ cup = 150 mL
$3/4$ cup = 175 mL
1 cup = 250 mL
2 cups = 1 pint = 500 mL
3 cups = 750 mL
4 cups = 1 quart = 1 L

VOLUME MEASUREMENTS (fluid)

1 fluid ounce (2 tablespoons) = 30 mL
4 fluid ounces ($1/2$ cup) = 125 mL
8 fluid ounces (1 cup) = 250 mL
12 fluid ounces ($1 1/2$ cups) = 375 mL
16 fluid ounces (2 cups) = 500 mL

WEIGHTS (mass)

$1/2$ ounce = 15 g
1 ounce = 30 g
3 ounces = 90 g
4 ounces = 120 g
8 ounces = 225 g
10 ounces = 285 g
12 ounces = 360 g
16 ounces = 1 pound = 450 g

DIMENSIONS

$1/16$ inch = 2 mm
$1/8$ inch = 3 mm
$1/4$ inch = 6 mm
$1/2$ inch = 1.5 cm
$3/4$ inch = 2 cm
1 inch = 2.5 cm

OVEN TEMPERATURES

250°F = 120°C
275°F = 140°C
300°F = 150°C
325°F = 160°C
350°F = 180°C
375°F = 190°C
400°F = 200°C
425°F = 220°C
450°F = 230°C

BAKING PAN SIZES

Utensil	Size in Inches/Quarts	Metric Volume	Size in Centimeters
Baking or Cake Pan (square or rectangular)	8×8×2	2 L	20×20×5
	9×9×2	2.5 L	23×23×5
	12×8×2	3 L	30×20×5
	13×9×2	3.5 L	33×23×5
Loaf Pan	8×4×3	1.5 L	20×10×7
	9×5×3	2 L	23×13×7
Round Layer Cake Pan	8×1½	1.2 L	20×4
	9×1½	1.5 L	23×4
Pie Plate	8×1¼	750 mL	20×3
	9×1¼	1 L	23×3
Baking Dish or Casserole	1 quart	1 L	—
	1½ quart	1.5 L	—
	2 quart	2 L	—